DAVID IGNATOW: Poems 1934–1969

DAVID IGNATOW
Poems 1934–1969

WESLEYAN UNIVERSITY PRESS

Middletown, Connecticut

Copyright© 1946, 1948, 1953, 1954, 1955, 1956, 1957, 1958, 1959, 1960, 1961, 1962, 1963, 1964, 1965, 1966, 1967, 1968, 1969, 1970 by David Ignatow.

Many of these poems have previously appeared elsewhere. For permission to reprint and for assigning copyrights to him, the author is grateful to the editors and publishers of the following:

Abraxas, American Dialogue, American Poetry Magazine, Antioch Review, Antioch Review Anthology, Athanor, Beloit Poetry Journal, Between Worlds, Botteghe Oscure, Cafe Solo, Carleton Miscellany, Chelsea, Chicago Jewish Forum, Choice, Cloud Marauder, Commentary, December, Discovery 1, Elizabeth, Epoch, The Fifties, Floating World, Frostbite, Golden Goose, Grist, IT, Inside Outer Space (Doubleday & Company, Inc.), *Jewish Frontier, kayak, Labor Zionist News, Midstream, The Midstream Reader, The Nation, New Orleans Poetry Journal, New American Review, New Mexico Quarterly, New World Writing, The New York Times, North American Review, Perspective, The Poetry Bag, Pogamoggan, Quarterly Review of Literature, Saturday Review, Sequoia, The Seventies, The Sixties, Some/Thing, Southern Review, Sou'wester, Tennessee Poetry Journal, The Stieglitz Memorial Portfolio* (Dorothy Norman: Twice a Year Press), *12th Street Quarterly, University of Tampa Poetry Review, Village Voice, Voices, War Resisters League 1968 Peace Calendar, Yale Review.*

"Sediment" appeared originally in *The New Yorker.*

"All Quiet," "And Step," "Beautiful and Kind," "For Nobody Else," "The Hope," "I Felt," "If My Hand," "Job's Anger," "Like Smoke," "The Mountain Is Stripped," "On the Death of Winston Churchill," "Rescue the Dead," "A Semblance," and "To Nowhere" were first printed in *Poetry.*

To Robert Bly, Sandy MacIntosh, Sonia Raiziss, Armand Schwerner, Harvey Shapiro, and J. R. de la Torre Bueno I owe a lasting debt which I hope is evident in each of these pages. My wife's contribution is beyond measurement.

SBN 8195 4014 5

Library of Congress Catalog Card Number: 79-105500

Manufactured in the United States of America

FIRST EDITION

Contents

PART SIX : *from* Say Pardon *(1961)*

PART ONE

Poems of the 1930's

Three

Coming to you
I was afraid the train might stop.
I was afraid, crossing the street.
I had no fear yet of bombs.

In any case, I hoped
they'd let you know,
as I'd have begged them.
                    •
You have your mother's brow,
and your mother's chin.
Your mother makes quiet moves
and her children love her.
                    •
Fruit I love, soft, sweet;
hard and sweet, or citrus
that chides the palate.
Your eyes are like blue fruit,
blue grapes I remember
that spilled wine.

Origins

While you offer me smiles I submit poems
for your pleasure.
                    What was your question
at the door, about to let me pass? "And is that
        all?"
I who never dreamt it, added, reading your smile,
"I write poems."
                    And at home, haunted by my reply,
slowly worked it towards truth, turning
the vehicle of my wealth in your direction:
my words, my rhythms. I have abandoned
the black satin road in which the world is laid.

My mistress, by a smile in your domain of silence
I am chosen to come forward
in a suspended mist of your delight.

Pardon Keeps the Sun

You say sorrow and desperation
and my thinking stays on your face.
I want to touch you,
though I know you are a problem to yourself.
I put my arms around you
and have your resistance.
You blame your life
but it is you I hold.
You make an effort to be free,
turning in my arms.

.

Let me praise the one life we lead,
with little to spare for one another.
It is difficult to smile.
We have decided this could be the goal,
and when we die there is this
to convince us, that death could not
possibly have come unless fulfillment
had been reached before.

.

Content in your love, I feel a pressure
upon it. I recognize that force
and am afraid. It was the voice
that broke up the singing
games when I was a child, and death
that stood inside a dream
when I was a boy
or the loud laugh of lies
when I grew up

.

Before parting we kissed,
but have I said or did I act
the slightest tick upon your happiness;
at which in your aloneness you point,
making a character of that tick,
making your love point like a weathervane
towards a harsh wind?
Remember in proportion,
I must be sure of no change.

.

Now you have loved,
now you sit sewing
and thinking.
Where is the connection?
What boisterous sense
must I invoke
to understand?
Evil keeps hinting
it is a song
starting in the lower scale
after the long climax.

.

No passage for work, my arms
lie upon the desk like logs
sogged with rain. I am unable
to take up pen and work,
for I have done to us, as though
I had scratched a mirror.
I am so charged with longing to go to you,
to plead with what beauty of me is left
to muster that I am more to be forgiven
than berated; which mood only again
scratches the bright day between us,
but pardon keeps the sun.

.

It's mostly what you have to offer me
who am very weak in certain things.
Our eyes meet and I feel I am known
to you.

But in my cunning
I think something in yourself
needs me with my failures.

.

Mostly
I have thrust lever beneath hindrance,
writing to you: urging from between
that which is only us. Made lines
the concrete of my speech
to fasten your hope of me.
Today, all clear between us,
I move upon the seacalm of your lips
like a ship on quiet bay.
I hold a glad and quiet watch.

Adolescence

I too have been drawn in
by a silken cord hung from her waist,
my form clapped to hers
and freedom restrained to our movement together.
Caught and the fields at our backs
we look past each other's face
but see our stretched necks
and taut cheeks straining.

Is this the love I ran after,
crying to it to turn
and catch me up? Whoever I chased
ran over the length of the world.

Pale Skin

Pale skin is upon the cheekbone like a plea,
making the hollows wide scoops of sadness.

Her eyes are slow, but her laugh
is still running from me. She has nestled
her mind at her husband's chest, and laid
the cover of stolidity across them.
She starves on the bare bone, and sweats.
She has put on her husband's thoughts,
and freezes; but she is entranced,
intimidated by the pomp of wealth.
I only have her love, her husband
asks her desires.

An Evening

An evening in the wind, in the fruitless heart of
    fruit. Amen.
We walk in trouble. I am kin to the sightless
    animals.
I am aware of the consequences; the sleek,
    the bleeding cheek.
Therefore, O let me raise a trumpet in the moon-
    light, my outspread shadow.
Pass to me, through shades of songs, consternation.

The Folk Singer

The other day I heard in the movies
a man sing a song, just like he told
your own troubles; he sang so beautiful,
just like you feel it,
it was just like in life: your ambitions
when you're young, and end up
in a shoe store; it was so good,

and everybody clapped
as if he could hear from the screen,
it was so beautiful
how he sang.

Autumn Leaves

Children of the road, autumn leaves,
forced from once well-stocked homes,
what depression has shriveled their sources?
What supply and demand dropped them:
yellowed with ragged edges, mobs
over the whole land; mouldering
on streets, crumbling on windswirls?
Have they left their homes for good,
comrades to spring, frost's victims?

·

God stalks by stubble fields
in a shivering garment of brown, wrinkled leaves,
at the heels mud, on His face the weather,
and in His hand a bunch of unripened torn-up
     grain.
God, like a shriveled nut where plumpness
and the fruit have fed the worm,
lies sprawled beneath a tree,
gaunt in His giving.

For a Friend

I did not tell you to open the window
when the sun shines. I asked for an old man
near a tattered cart selling luck charms.
But tell me, what is the truth,
what is the music in the box
when bananas fall from stars?

I would not peel a stinking egg
if I were you, Columbus, O Gem of the ocean.
Make it stand without breaking.

I said the rain was running against the curb
and the clop of hooves in the air,
fuzzy light, wet walks;
your clothes all wet.
I said you must not turn your back
nor take away your hands.
Your must not humph, nor drop your clothes from
     you
and leave the room.
          You left and not even a handshake
while the factory whistled come to work.
I turned in bed going over the ground with you
and agreeing. In the dawn I rose
looking for needle and thread.
I found a dime in the street.

Interior Dialogue

I count the sidewalk slits,
pacing in mind two at a stride.
Therefore, eat your pie before it stales.
But that is dropping the milk!
How shall we feed the babies?
Lots of opinions on that, I'd say.
Just snap your suspenders and wink.
Others might want to grab a hammer.
I'm not for it.
Maybe I'd be, if you dropped me.

I've changed my mind, you see.
Very funny, forgetting in the second verse

that I was not going fast enough in the first.
Don't you drink your coffee that way too?
Of course you do!

Who says?

Forks with Points Up

Points up, our forks;
past ceilings, with the going to bed,
and all night unlace our shoes with thought.
No water falls from fingertips,
but moons, pasted labels,
we walking around the block three times,
fingers crossed, or playing dolls,
for the stars will go out
and we shall go visiting,
patting on our hip a pistol,
shake hands with mummies, dig sewers,
make money or puke in the street,
bent from the waist down, groaning.

No hand run through it, no rose in your hair,
no smoke or bombardments;
choose your nearest exit;
say no and drink it down from a shaving cup;
let your beard grow, pull on it thoughtfully,
your belly shaking with laughter.
Try turning to the next page.

Neighbors

Where do they find the answers?
Never have I heard shouting or violent noise
from the windows across the street. Lights

and music, some loud talk, glasses tinkling
and cigar smoke trailing out of the windows.
I will not say perfect lives,
I have heard of the death of a daughter
in childbirth. The tears and laments
were hard to listen to; people closed
their windows and wiped their brows.

The grandmother sits silently
with the newborn on the stoop.
Here is quiet and ability to dress
and undress, to eat and to digest,
to expel waste and to make arrangements
and to carry them out.

My Neighbor

Why is that old woman in the gutter,
dressed in her kitchen clothes,
a cloth upon her head to keep off the dust?
See, it's night and it's cold
and the street is empty.
Up and down the gutter she looks,
holding in both hands a motionless rug.
She flaps it once and twice, then pauses.
Now she is trotting out of the way
of an oncoming car and shouts after it,
shaking her fist. The driver must be amused,
but the next one might yell,
"Get on the sidewalk where you belong!"

For My Mother Ill

I'll join you in your sleep,
into the same darkness dive,

where dead fish float together.
But we shall be communing,
blindly and without feeling;
but by knowing now,
as I lie back upon a pillow,
as you close your eyes,
the comfort of it.

PART TWO
Poems of the 1940's

Droll Husband

Whatever this world means to me,
it does not go beyond you
at a kitchen stove.

You take a dollar and make it grow
vegetables and fruit for a week.
What is in the palm of your hand
that gives a shabby bill the power
of a handful of seed
or that brings home the whole cow,
it seems?

And at table I hear music
of the smacking of your lips
over soup, so that my stomach
cannot listen without swooning;
and conversation, veritably
a holy book, which for its beauty
I must study—your conquests
in the market every day.

Indeed, then, shall I not ponder
such revelation like a prayer
before food? Am I not blessed
to the edge of life? I may sit down
beneath a lamp and discuss calmly
with my newspaper the world's ills.

Consolation

My wife, I dread to come and tell you
how we've failed. It is not our doing
wholly. What has gone out of us
is the impelling reason to succeed,
to set ourselves above others,
to live more perfectly. All this

has left us as though we too
had been possessed of a fever,
and our minds now turning cool
have revealed to us our arms
enclosed about each other.

At Home

See how it takes us, my finished darling,
as you leave me in another room.
Do you go away an old woman for us both
and we were young and high up
and I have come to the level of things
down I have scorned. Was I once
a favorite but have you to think me old
and yourself in my eyes a stooped figure?

We go away in shapes of stone and tree
and I have dreamt and you have heard me say
them all in the morning and in the evening
and that tears are for nothing.

Marriage

We are waiting in separate rooms
with doors closed between us.
In the desire to be apart is the wish
to renew ourselves to each other
and so we sit each alone
with nothing to do, really,
for we are all there is to do,
our rooms silent.
                We listen
to boys in the street
boisterous on a night out.

•

Our life together has been to shore up good
against evil, to keep us from being flooded apart,
to keep land beneath us: to stem the onrush
of more evil mounting with spite of guilt;
to place a soft wall, evil subsiding against it
in sleep, reproachful sleep that turns
to flowered dreams breathing deeply upon softness.
And we have succeeded, by being a wall to each
    other,
to keep us from flooding ourselves with the fiery
and omnivorous.
                  We wave to one another
from the ramparts,
with no man's land between.

             .

You sat across the table and drew pictures,
perhaps of me or of others with us;
you cannot recall, here now bound to me
in marriage. With such mystery is time filled.

I approached from around the table,
smiling, my curiosity to this day
unfilled. What did we do to bring us
together, you smiling at me in return?
A mystery in which we are held
side by side, because it cannot be answered
by a few phrases about love.

I lie here, my thoughts restful
as if life were moving to some haven,
and getting up to find food
for my stomach with the passing hours,
I say, protesting to myself,
But I have lived.

Physical Love

I would like to know which way does it curl
and of what thickness and color
and does one get the impression of a gloomy entrance
looking down at it and does one think
of being lost in the gloom where the hair thins off
to show beneath the pale skin what has been
too long in darkness? Shall one wander in that
pale field and be happy and know all
the sensation and then plunge abruptly down
into its entrance, thick strewn with curls
and find choking excitement, the compressed
atmosphere, the moist density, the tense lack
of air of a cavern, and wildly, so much afraid,
so much elated, explore by wall probing
where does this lead, what lies at the bottom
and shall one be bitten off at the head,
to be plunged in darkness without ever being able
to remember light again? Sweet terror drives me
on, my action more violent as with driving
onwards I grow more explicitly for joy.
In the depths is no resistance and my own beating
joy at the bottom awaits me and with my consent
swallows me.

Memories of a Horseman

I am never so quick as when I ride
nor half so lithe as when I lean
far over in the saddle and race
over the shrub plain, leaping
the hedgerows, the legs of my mount
soaring, I hold on at those moments;
we are together in this;
and when we come down,
hooves taking the ground rapidly,

my senses returned, I hear
pounding on to the next rise.
I hold the reins loose around the neck,
my knees again guiding, my breath restored;
my stamina, that hurdle cleared, revived.

On and on we ride, I leaning far over
to cut the wind's force and to ride
alert, agile and adept. The race run,
we do not have to catch our fox
nor hear the hounds bay. I dismount,
straightening up to feel the sky
once more resisting my head.

We Are Reliving Dead Men's Lives

The club in the hand of the forest prowler
is now in the cop's hand, and the car we drive
is the elephant we rode through the jungles,
and the woman we marry and have children with
is she who years ago forced us to settle
in one cave; we saw sunlight ahead
in a clearing, but she refused to budge
and had her children in the hidden dark.

The love we have built up
and will see torn down,
not by our hand but by the gravedigger,
is the cry that was heard
in the forest when we were gored;
she saw us fall under the beast
and ran and hid herself in our cave
to have it alone, for we are
reliving dead men's lives.

Lovers

The sea drills into the shore,
the shore repels it stubbornly
from the mainland, indifferent and swollen.
The sea has the leaping shark of its ferocity.
They meet head on in a clash of temperament.
The sea withdraws, stunned; the land stays,
bruised, dented. They understand each other,
the sea lashing out again,
the land murmuring nothing of its bruises.

Though they understand each other,
they will not have each other
for a moment, the land abundant,
the sea fluid with anger.
Not to have each other
and not to submit to that either,
the sea dragging parts down into its depths;
what remains behind wet with pleasure.

Not to have each other
and not to know each other;
except as enemy. The sea roars
its loneliness upon the shore,
the land harbors its bruises,
rises to great heights of forgetfulness
and descends steeply to its own true state
upon the plains. It cannot maintain
long the ecstasy, though left behind
in still form.

The waves, towering above the land's edge,
are a statement of limits.
The sea lies restlessly beyond,
sending ahead new probes. In this
then must be its pleasure,
for as long as the moon draws it with love
to the limit.

The Murderer

I pull a knife but it is to protest
a loss. I am not allowed to love
that person who has made me angry.
Is this then what he wants?
He has this blade to find out his heart;
and those who cart me off to jail,
I love them too
for the grief and anger
I have given.

Money and Grass

1.

Tonight reality is in the rest
I have found from murdering myself
racing through streets,
my mind racing ahead,
my body pounding after
money—green as grass!

No time to think of grass!
No time to think of lying under a tree,
watching people far off in a slow-motion
drama towards each other.

And so I find at end of day my mind
going around like an idle phonograph
with drunken hiccups where the record's cracked,
my body still racing upon a couch,
the blood whirring, the nerves ringing,
the legs seeming afloat with a striding motion,
at rest on a whirlwind
and find my senses clouded
from ordinary faces, from simple food,
from plain, cheerful talk.
I cannot grasp any of it

as I lie idle; and I know
this is murder of myself
evaporating as a tingle, my whole body
compressed for the energy to make
an electric shock, then dropped
like a vibrating doll.

2.

But tonight,
I have stuffed wax into my ears
to keep out the trucks and auto horns
in the street. I listen to my blood
ringing until it sounds like crickets
in a woods at night. I am quieted,
listening to my own isolation,
myself rooted in the compact,
the quality of earth held in a full hand,
the silkiness, the tiny workworms,
the little stones and the rootbeer deliciousness
of the earth itself, brown, black or red
for growing.
I feel through my cricket-singing
blood and rest my underlying constant affair
with earth, with its trees that are tall
and pregnant to express love, and the grass
running with the wind: the happiness
one must bring to love and the clumps
of flower bushes the occasional monuments
one must leave to love. I feel love only
can be justice, and the earth grow it.

I feel never to leave this perfect lover,
and roll upon it with the abandonment
of a lover on his mistress' body.
I get up renewed in having released myself,
the tiredness and tingling gone with it,
and I am earth's offering again
to wild horns and engines.

Like Smoke

The ground, the apartment house
that stands upon it, the haze
from too much sun upon the roof
and the sky in its simple blue
are tranquil with their meaning
that the slow drifting chimney smoke
on this windless day expresses.

A well-being
that takes its own path
touched by a current of air,
by something solid.
It spreads itself around and about
modestly, like smoke
going up.

Day My Dream

Fish tossed on sand,
flopping for air; overhead
two-legged people stride about.
Such a scene is normal to me.

Deer hunted through the woods,
heads high in terror. Men train
normal guns on them.
                    The explosive
mouth that fragments the atmosphere;
the old woman who drools on a bus
crowded with intensely dressed salesmen.
How they look away in disgust.
All this is normal to me,
as the face in my mirror each morning—
lined by guilt of the night;
lips relaxed from rightness, creases
under the eyes enfolding pleasure

in dark folds.
                    Since the tunnel
in which I have acted out my dreams
has been lit with these passions,
revealing my form, I converse with all,
as if night were day and my dream.

And He Will Fail

I have been assaulted, met in a dark alley
on the way home with a salary of a week's work.
Out of the dark stepped one hidden
by a handkerchief across his face.
What, anonymous? And struck a personal blow?
Is there such an issue against earning
one's living?
                    As the news is flashed
it is felt in Africa among the warning,
wailing drums. "There are evil forces
at work among us. One has made his rightful
earnings and been robbed. What is good, then?
What is lifelike and urgent?"
The tom-toms wail and warn, confused
about events. The grain threshed in the sun,
the alligator rivers risked for turtle food—
is it all a mistake? Is the spear
the progenitor of life? The women have ceased
to knead the bread of the threshed grain,
and have sat down to wait with the tom-toms.
Nothing is being readied for tomorrow's mouth.
which shall feed on their livers and fat tissue
because Tomorrow will be hungry
and they will sit wan and wondering.

What an attack upon life so flimsy
in its being. A solid, anonymous blackjack
has found a way to crush it. But the tom-toms

and the wailers rise up just as angrily
as the power that dealt the blow,
for it was recognizable force.
And he will fail!

Marketing

The noise is not enough,
I must have the bargains:
the fishmonger's bloody package
at the price. I suffer it
with shaking hands.

The clothier's bargain to fit me,
having woven the cloth. I am
exhausted, hold me up,
bracket me in a fine suit:
return me my labor,
I die moral.

The White Ceiling

Until that child, one flight below, stops crying,
struck by its mother, I cannot sleep—
until it is hushed up by kindness,
a stroke silently, softly given upon its head.
Why not, I think, go downstairs in my bathrobe,
knock gently on the door and ask permission,
"If you don't mind," so that I too
may sleep.
               There was an argument
between parents about money; not altogether;
their voices personal as money is not.
In the hush of an unhappy truce the slap sounded.

Since those below are helpless, I lie here
and look up at the white ceiling.

The Theory of Dressing

These shoes are for these lines,
and any feature I discern in them
is for the betterment of these lines.
Our ways are one in street and house,
and these lines, insisting upon shoes,
are my thoughts of them.

My needs,
not to be neglected, are reflected
in my lines. Will you say
I have ignored what is greater,
my happiness, when we fit together,
my shoes and I?

A Working Principle

Let them go around on tiptoes,
craning their necks for the ineffable
in the driving rain, as flatfooted and slow,
I make my way, unable to pretend
as others do, maddened at the prospect
before them, that beauty calls them
from within. I will end in the mud,
face down, saying the night is dark.
They will say, Black is merely the absence
of color.

·

Poets I have refused to read
who remind me of my misery,
for there is nothing else
to address the world

that moves like a cloud of elephants,
and every person's identity
is by his own stomping.

So many people are dead
or dying that I begin to think
it must be right;
and so many are
crowding into the world
that living too
must be worth while.

Epilogue for FDR

How shall we forget your smile
or the bold lift of your arm
or the witticism that pinned your foe?
The first bombs stunned you,
and in the raining shells you grew cool.
We left our farms and cities
to make a phalanx across the land,
closed ranks; and your flowing cape,
once tossed by the wind, lay crushed
between khaki shoulders.

The mourners are marching in uniform
by the millions, thick as lava.
You had spoken of freedom
and man's share in his brother's joy.
We shouldered your beliefs,
lived them by your practical score,
and heard your voice, humorous, direct.
The talents lived for you, the artist
painting hungry faces and a promise;

the writer narrating death
and reporting hope; the dancer
calling up misery and want,
relaxing in love by a body motion;
philosophers, politicians, union men
devising ideas for the fact
and acting upon your good humour,
and insight.

The guns thumping softly in the night,
they were betraying you, pounding holes
in the dark through which air rushed,
escaping, leaving a vacuum for your voice.
We were still, caught each in our separate life,
one with an arm lifted to the sky,
another pointing to earth and to men.
Many were carrying their belongings
or their work in their arms, and all turned,
hearing the air escape, the guns thumping.
And your voice hardened in the vacuum;
our bodies grew taut; our thoughts,
our lives and work heavy as weapons.
Your casket upon a gun carriage,
we too were still.

Dream of practical love, go by,
drawn by white horses, trained haulers
of guns, our love speaking
to other guns.

We Came Naked

"On a level with your eyes, as far as that,
the land is yours".
                    We came naked
the ash smell upon us. We could believe
it our bodies; no soul stirred in us—

blackened tongues wilted upon the ground.
We believed we were dead and in hell,
piled bodies aspiring before us.
Although we speak with the tongue of a witness,
a voice we do not know from the fires, crackling.

Pray by every flame you strike, the dreaming coal.
We were fuel ripped from our homes: slats
heaped for their hatred. Our souls dissolved
from us upon the ground, our faith in tears.

What did we believe in then,
our homes but emblems of the enemy?

To you, then, steering by David's star
into Jerusalem's heart, our soul!
Of the hot sun and frank foliage!
Figures that passed each heap of ourselves
along the cindered path green, setting foot
upon your outstretched hand, Jerusalem!
In your streets feeding us history,
beyond the gates the mountains, valleys, plains,
in their shawls of drab land
praying for us; and brought them joy
throwing their mantles off to know us
once more; feasted each other over the table
of the land. What food! No feat of love
between us too difficult! We died
in each other's arms over and over,
to rise at memory of the joys.

The Longest Knives

In a garden of innocent instruments,
wheels for baby carriages, springs
for beds, we roamed. Orders
from all over the world! One thousand

diaper pins for Argentina. Those
we sent posthaste. No grenade pins,
no! One thousand cans of milk for China
we sent by rocket plane. Not cans
of liquid fire, never! Our garden
was hung with pictures of the blest,
who prospered from our pride: baby carriage
bed spring milk bottle makers together
with recipients of their wares:
fed children from China, contented folk in Argentina.
We are so innocent, we do not even know why!

We played in our garden, expecting
other children, and as we peeked across
the garden wall and climbed over
to join others at play
we were struck down.

Call in the Children's Aid Society!
Fill our hands with the longest knives!
An attempt has been made on our innocent lives!

Mirrors

Finish your food, as the shell strikes
in another country, and tie up
your small bundle of papers.
At first warning siren, straighten
your tie and run into the underground.
It will not suit to sit as you do
in your room; prepare another world
of pastures and fences and tall buildings
to be bombed, and you running
with your small bundle of papers.

Birthday

Today being the day, what gift can I give
myself, earth giving none, nor my nearest
relative? I take the gift of coming bombs.
We shall all be dead on a certain day.
I take my last few looks at the surrounding
scene: stone buildings, hard pavements,
noisy streets, trees dying
of carbon dioxide.
                    May I live to see
this last bomb flower
in the paradise we promised to each other.

Independence

The child he raises in the slums;
the sixth-floor walkup where the small radiator
sputters against the iron cold; the little job
at which he can assert himself, threatening
to quit—it pays so little; old and broken-
down shoes to which he routinely changes
after work, to save wear on the new—
he looks upon this domain proudly:
his wife in a housecoat five years shabby,
who will come to surprise her in it?
The pants, new and well pressed,
that lie untouched in a special drawer
till pride requires them; the long view
of the city from top floor—people
who relax in penthouses see
hardly more.

The Clinic

Poor slobs, who warm their bottoms
on wood, while doctor adjusts
his nstruments between calls
for luncheon appointments—
and no man should neglect phoning
his family at least twice a day.
While these in patched underwear
wait depressed on the pauper's bench;
perhaps, if not too far gone in spirit,
count the money they could make
if they were not so broke
they must wait meekly
for help.

Subway

There slouched the drunk, head fallen
to a side, arms hung down. I strode by
to take a seat farther up the train
though I was tired and had determined
to be settled in the first vacancy.
I kept walking, revolted. Here all day
I had worked to make better a portion
of my life—to find him at my feet.
I should have sat down opposite
and confessed that if this day
really were bettered by my efforts
he could not deter me.

Premonitions

A bird winging through space
you love for the distance

it soars and circles,
in time.

                    ·

In places where the sun does not reach,
as in a shady room, time presses again
upon the forehead. In a field
under a shade of a tree it comes
softly to rest upon your head.
You dread the first sight
of the going down of the sun,
the air melancholy over the fields,
the sky thoughtful and subdued upon the hills,
the trees prominent and stark.
But this melancholy you enjoy,
feeling its richness of the sun,
is time again, I think, returning
to sympathize with us.
                    For time,
I begin to believe, is the earth
pressing upwards against our feet
to make our heads feel it.
Earth may be time that the sun softens,
its message that we are one.

Time then is the warning of death to come,
pressing upon us in a shaded room
or under a shady tree and at night
when the sun must leave us to darkness,
for the sun too by this token
is in time's control.
               Then time
has its deceptions for us as in the sun
and we are time itself running its course,
and when we are done time remains,
for it is the earth and we are dying
to be born into the world again
for we are thoughts of time
and our shapes too are time

and because all things are one
with their differences which add up to time.

And so we are not alone dying
and not alone being born,
for we have earth's weight urging upon us
in one pressure of life and death.
Time then for us is a standing still in abundance,
so much so that it is all
and we are in eternity.
And what we do for now is for always,
as what we have done is the future too
which is always.

PART THREE
from Poems *(1948)*

To Rose, my wife

Statement for the Times

On Sunday, day of rest, visiting the lake
and the ducks in it, I look at the hills
in the distance in another state.
I go home, I go to war
with my ambition against my mind.

The larger wars are for the masses.
We shall burn down the cities,
and build them up again.
We shall burn them down again,
and be damned for it,
for a stubborn ideal.

Brooding

The sadness of our lives.
We will never be good enough to each other,
to our parents and friends.
We go along like old sailing ships,
loaded with food and drink for a long voyage,
self-sufficient, without any outside contact
with the world as they sailed.

The truth faces me all the time.
We are in a world in which nobody listens to
    anybody,
in which we do as we please until we are stopped
by others. We live our whole lives as in a husk,
like an ear of corn. The husk is our will,
which keeps us separate from any influence,
while those influenced are idiots
or people without consciousness.

Peace for Awhile

Peace for awhile,
but there is no such thing as peace forever.
The calm suburbs you see
while passing by on a train,
the children riding their bikes under trees,
are only interludes between the strain
of coming to grips with what we wish to do
and the failure to do it.

To a Friend Who Has Moved to the East Side

What did you expect you were getting?
You were moving in among drunks and workers:
men who would pass you by on a stairway at
    night
in silence, leaving you to think
that they had taken note,
and next time would know how to attack.
Men with bristling chins and broad jaws,
with dark complexions, looking like the type
used in the movies to depict a foreign hoodlum
attacking our women.
You were coming among people who work for a
    living,
and look angry about it too.
Do you want to work each day except Sunday
at hard manual labor?

My friend must know that he has moved
into such a neighborhood because he had to,
not because it pleased him to be different
or to defy the conventions of a world
he was leaving. He must know that he would find
the people no different than himself,
even if they are lying drunk in the halls.

You, my friend, are drunk on self-approval,
but they are drunk on their forgetfulness;
trying to forget
what you have yet to learn.
They are looking for the peace that must come
of the hard facts, while you are weaving
like a tipsy dancer in a dream of self-love.

You have made me ashamed of you,
and ashamed of myself for having tried to hide
the facts.
You have made me afraid
you would not be able to take the truth.
You have made me lie, pretending
we were on a gay excursion of a colorful scene.
"The neighborhood was drab,
but the rooms were charming.
All the best people were taking rooms in such places."
Shall you be my true friend?

Nocturne

My room is lit, and those who care
to look in may see me sitting
at my window. And so I may
look into the windows of others,
giving warning to those
who like to hide.
                    I am looking
for life when emotions are sordid.
I should be thrilled
that moment when human passes
into beast, to distinguish the difference.
                    .

Ugly is the word
and do not be scared of mirrors.
The sewer runs through the neatest block,

the tide carrying crud and contraceptives,
and I have thoughts to make the hair
of strangers stand on end.
                              We are together
by contact of our hands on furniture,
books, plates and fruits of the corner peddler's
busiest intersection.

Poem

I am tired of you
as I am tired of myself.
There is a mountain I am climbing
in the dark,
and when I reach its top
the dark will be there.

Tenderness

Tenderness I have for good gifts, chant the women.
Sweet clothes, perfume, high heels and brocades.
Who do you come from with tenderness, they ask,
when we do not love ourselves enough to love you?
Whom are you in love with that you can love us?
Are you self-satisfied?
Hide such hideousness in ornament and battle:
man loving himself, fornicating with him,
circling like a dog swallowing his own tail.
Now leave us for fighting and for fortune,
for folly and crime, spoke all the women.
They danced the symbols of finery and conceit:
long arms like snakes and legs in motion
like the hind parts of a dog.

Tenderness we have for small wrist watches
encrusted with sparkle and gilt, for earrings
and long-stemmed flowers.
We hide from lovers who come to love,
let them come shielded in good suits
and hats, long cigars and canes twirling,
eyes arrogant to take us.

I loved as they intended, and laughed.
I was with all and was forgotten as any other.
Out of the tunnel I crept, no longer myself,
without tenderness, without love,
too tired to kill, killed too often in return.
Willing to wait, hoping to love by armed truce.
Their snake-filled arms beckon to me,
for there is no other grace in the world
but the bloodshed deed, beautiful
for its loneliness.

Park

I sit beside old retired Italians.
They chat and have smooth skins.
Their hair is white, and the flesh full.
They make no disturbance.
They rest all day, sitting in a park.
One will come over from his house
and add to the crowd.
                    They never
grow loud. They talk and laugh,
solid company every day. I love
to come here and sit with them,
I a stranger, and feel the quiet
and stability they make,
and lasting custom.

At the Zoo

We have locked up the elephant,
and giggly children feed him peanuts
through the bars. But he can live on straw,
swaying his delicate feeler from side to side
to pick, like the arm of a dancer in a dance.

Nothing can keep the elephant from himself
and he who locked him up comes back
to look through bars, and mourn
the stingy space and concrete setting
for an elephant.

In My Room

If my wife thinks I am sitting here being ambitious,
it is very funny.
I am sitting here
doing exactly what would shock the world.
I am sitting in a most comfortable pose
doing nothing.

No ambition and no high thought.
No yearning to save the world
or to be saved by it.
Let me do as I please
and I shall harm no one.
Keep me from doing what I want
and I shall harm someone,
including myself.

The Poet Is a Hospital Clerk

What I am trying to say is this:
why did I call up the nurse
to chase down the woman visiting her daughter
who had just given birth?
Why did I chase her down?
She had a right to be there,
at the birth of her first grandson.
Couldn't I have let her stay?
Sure I could have let her stay.
Haven't I let others do the same?
Why did I not let her see her grandchild,
when I could feel her feelings?

Because there was a mean canker in me,
a mean streak that comes from bitterness.
From bitterness that comes from disappointment.
From disappointment that comes from frustration.
From frustration that comes from weakness.
From weakness that comes from character.
From character that comes from fears.
From fears that come from cowardice.
From cowardice that comes from a small mind.

And so I let her wait.
And so I made her suffer.
And so I made her feel the way I feel.
I who was looking for fame and glory,
for public leadership, for world acclaim,
for great stature as man and artist,
the greatest yet. Me? Jerk?
Man with nothing to brag about?

I have said it before, I am no good.
I am a jumble of pretense.
I am nonsense shot through with lies and self-
    deception.
Don't I know who I am?

I hold up a mirror to myself and laugh.
What a fool I am.
Do you always fall for the same boasting
and bragging, the same dream of greatness?
Is it not true it never sounds sincere
when you talk of better things to come?
Is it not true you sound more convincing
when you laugh and ridicule yourself,
when you deride and abuse and hate yourself?
Are you not more sure when you talk
of yourself as a failure?

Then you will know what you are talking about.
Laugh at yourself.
You might not even succeed
in talking about yourself as a failure.
You may yet put in the falsest vanities.
You are just a plain no-good failure,
and remember it, just plain.
Why, you even think of writing poetry
at this moment. Don't you realize
the depth of your debasement?

Hate yourself. It might save you.
It might keep you on the level,
having lived in humility and self-distrust.
An ordinary man is a message to the world:
Produce, and be silent.
You may have some dignity in your own eyes,
for you are not being fooled by your small worth.

Do you think you have genius?
Do you think you are entitled to a special consideration?
Have no mercy on yourself.
You are the typical man with illusions of grandeur.
Remember your defeat and be humble.
Take your last rites like a dying man.
In your smallness all that you can do
is to be decent about it.

Show a good front.
Remember, be nice, you pompous fool,
you self-deceiver, you crybaby crab.
Show a good face. March to your death.
In memory of yourself, in sorrow be good to others.
Remember how it hurts to be counted out.
Save that much of your self-respect, your honor,
by being good, you loser.

Hospital Clerk

(For Walt Whitman)

How many whose names and addresses,
whose age and place of birth, taken
of their own lips, have died since?
I admit newborn babies too,
giving them their first tag number.

Poetry is to be written here,
among the deaths and births,
admitted by one clerk.
Have we become so deep and true here?

Stieglitz

Stieglitz wore a cap to taunt bulls
in his china shop, and those who were offended
had it thrown at them, with a smile.
Stieglitz at eighty wore it every day,
as much as any time when he was young,
and lacked only the strength to throw hard,
as he did them, but said, almost politely,
"Why don't you leave, if you don't like it?"

And no one left. Because they were offended,
and had to learn.
                    "Listen," he said one day,
lying on his couch in the back room. "Don't
excite me with new paintings at my age.
I'll take my stand on what I've found,
and let life be my ally for the future.
My pictures and my photographs will do something.
The way weakness hinders my own effort now
I am better dead. Then what I have done already
will be left to encourage others, whom I have no
        strength
to encourage now.
                    "And goodbye, bull,
in my china shop. Come back a lamb.
Even sell your business, you big broker.
Anyway, don't paint.
At least, just think a moment this:
To whom are you dictating, when you dictate?
Who is listening, telling you what
it takes to be wise,
and you have nothing but facts?
They are thrown into fire
and the fool snatches at the blaze.
Says the broker, 'Let him do it,
I won't.' And does nothing
and looks it."
                    Stieglitz, all ideas
came to one for you, lucky man.
You believed in and said, "Start
from any point and come towards the thorny bush
where Moses saw a God blaze. Let us
all see what we can, but with the heart in it.
All must be malleable in flame—
marble or stone or rock.
To the stake with all of you,
be light for the time you live."

Our Masterpiece

You can stick a sign For Sale
on the biggest part of America, the people.
Nobody will complain, only there isn't customer
wealthy enough for us, and so we sell in small
      lots
to each other.

America, America upon the dotted line,
and if we think we live purely on emotion,
go into any restaurant and see who flashes the
      wallet,
and who counts the change,
and who leaves embarrassed by his small tip.

I don't care what any man feels outside of business.
It plays as small a part as a bass fiddle
in a symphony. Blowhard trombone and French horn
are the money-makers,
and over all is the conductor, the idea of money
      itself,
pulling the song out of us, our masterpiece.

Hurry Hurry

Ay, open the window, the shop is stifling us:
the knocking folding machines,
the grit-grinding cutters.
Over the crash and roar we hear
the phone shriek, almost like our own insides—
as we stand wrapping the hours of paper packages
advertising toys, trinkets, polish,
objects that disappear beneath the hand,
leaving an empty can or bottle.

What does the woman-voiced phone want?
Another skid of folded leaflets selling
polish. Hurry, hurry: die quickly
of hunger or rush well fed worrying
into death.
         The sordid eye racing
around the walls is poisoned, the mouth
rotten with anxiety and speed. The rank
days bog down in rage and blue motor haze.

Harold

From the west comes Harold, with a bitter smile,
and a dry hate in his voice for micks, wops,
kikes and refugees.
         Too bad he has to work
in a Jewish hospital, admitting Jewish people,
sick or ready to give birth. He makes sure
not to raise his head while women suffer
before him as he writes slowly his data.
Or else how could he write home to the West,
to the tall sombreros and the spittin' type
that he, the climax of a pioneering dream,
works for Jews to make his bread?
Where is the gun he ought to pull
to plug them all, then swing off at a canter
for parts unknown till things cool off,
still master of his fate and fortune,
his own?
Here he mouths blasphemous phrases,
shocking his own Baptist soul. He makes free
with farts, shoots his jibes,
orders the help around.

He laces it into the assistant director,
the biggest, bloatiest doctor of them all,
and takes his something bucks a week disdainfully
for rent, food, gas to keep a car
and six-cent stamp for home.

Europe and America

My father brought the emigrant bundle
of desperation and worn threads,
that in anxiety as he stumbles
tumble out distractedly;
while I am bedded upon soft green money
that grows like grass.
Thus, between my father
who lives on bed of anguish for his daily bread,
and I who tear money at leisure by the roots,
where I lie in sun or shade,
a vast continent of breezes, storms to him,
shadows, darkness to him, small lakes, rough channels
to him, and hills, mountains to him, lie between
      us.

My father comes of a small hell
where bread and man have been kneaded and baked
      together.
You have heard the scream as the knife fell;
while I have slept
as guns pounded offshore.

Nurse

The old man who can undress before you
as easily as before a mirror believes
that you are only the matured concept of his body,
as idea only.

Let us hope your uniform does not deceive him,
in that you are dedicated to his care.
The dress you wear is white for the abolition
of all your woes before his;
for he has worn the body of his time
a little longer and a little more indulgently
than you, whose cries of welcome or goodby
beneath his window on your night leave
will wake him fitfully from the dream
of the burden of earth given back to earth again.

You are to know that body is love
of having been born and to grow old
is to be born into returning to the good
from which he came.
You have eyes to see no shame
but resignation in his stooped figure,
such as love brings.

And now, your own eyes are colorless of wrong,
and every look is to follow
one man's devotion to being old.
You take his clothes from him,
and let him rest;
and in your going to and fro
from cabinet to cot carry instruments
of your respect to his side.

Bowery

Bums are the spirit of us parked in ratty old hotels.
Bums are what we have made of angels,
given them old clothes to wear
dirty beards and an alcoholic breath,
to lie sprawled on gutters at our feet
as sacrifices to our idols: power and money.

Bums ask themselves, Why dress and shave,
and be well mannered, studious and hard-working,
own home and debts, a bank account and business
friends when others more eager are doing it
successfully? All we want is the right
to sit propped up against a wall, drunk
and drooling, letting urine seep through
our clothes onto the sidewalk, we
unconscious or unconcerned.
                                        We with no money
relax anyway, letting the world come in
on us in sidewalk spit on which we sprawl,
in kicks and jabs from cops, under open skies
in rain and snow. None of you dares do it,
and so you do not know what money means.
We who live on charity enjoy the pleasure
of your wealth, the long hours filled
with drunkenness.

Get the Gasworks

Get the gasworks in a poem
and you've got the smoke and smokestacks,
the mottled red and yellow tenements,
and grimy kids who curse with the pungency
of the odor of gas. You've got America, boy.

Sketch in the river, and barges,
all dirty and slimy.
How do the seagulls stay so white?
And always cawing like little mad geniuses?
You've got the kind of living
that makes the kind of thinking we do:
gaswork smokestack whistle tooting wisecracks.

They don't come because we like it that way,
but because we find it outside our window every
      morning,
in soot on the furniture,
and trucks carrying coal for gas,
the kid hot after the ball under the wheel.
He gets it over the belly, alright.
He lies there.

So the kids keep tossing the ball around
after the funeral.
So the cops keep chasing them,
so the mamas keep hollering,
and papa flings his newspaper outward,
in disgust with discipline.

She Was the Audience

The patriotic speeches,
the sentimental crude bombastic
tear-jerking windy promises;
and she, this woman with the baby,
this half-starved, half-crazy person
with no family and no money—
she was the audience,
holding her sickly baby.

The nights of moaning and shrieking
up and down the scale of hysteria;
from moans to alarming screams for help
at four in the morning, the husband entering
in disgust: the trouble, ignorance, no money,
apathy: she was the audience,
always too tired to take the child to the park
for sun; who never combed her own hair,
in wisps and straggles;
who could not walk without swaying from side to
        side,
as though half-drunk, maybe drunk with wondering,
suffering. She was the audience, holding up
her child, staring with a pleased smile at the noise,
the cheers, the speeches, the rouged quartets
singing bravura, the clapping for more.
She was the audience, with black dirty dress
hung on her like a board; torn shoes.

The public nurse she threw out of her house,
indignant at the need for public charity,
the stigma of poverty and ignorance;
the coarse strident pride;
the dark hole of a room
where the electric light was never off,
to keep out the dark;
where the washtub with its soapy stink was always
        present;
the brooms and rags and clothes piled in one heap;
the beds unmade from morning till night,
too tired to clean; the same black dress;
"What shall I do, what shall I do?"
He goes out. She must stay with the baby;
not even a carriage for it.
She was the audience.

The entertaining solicitor of war bonds
reminding them of their sex,
tying them to his speech by their sex;

throwing a few words of their language at them;
bringing a pretty girl to the front.
He gay and demanding, pirouetting, trulling
for their money, for the cause.
She was the audience, cursing all who asked her
to keep quiet during the night.
"Nobody cares for me! Why should I care for
        them!"
Her shrieking at a neighbor whom she accused
of sending the public nurse.
The fanfare ballyhoo circus for the cause:
liberty, democracy;
she was the audience.
"Fighting for what we take pride, glory in.
Cherish, honor, die for our country, our institutions!"
She was the audience
in wonder and pleasure
holding her baby up to the noise,
the enthusiasm, the crusade, the singing,
the gay chairman, the money pouring in
for bonds.

Come!

Come, let us blow up the whole business;
the city is insane.
Let us plant trees, grass and flowers
in the rubble to disguise it.
Let us restore the city to its first aim
of being natural to the touch.

Break down the sordid hospital,
the cockroach-ridden restaurants,
the whore-packed hotels
and business buildings close by for convenience;

the big night clubs and intimate ones
in the cellars of old homes,
where rats and vermin and dark dampness
used to sport.

The stock exchange and the banks
where we sell each other;
the gaudy apartment houses and the broken-down
        ones
to which we have been assigned,
each according to his profit;
the gutters where we run each other down;
the sidewalks where we watch with interest.
The stores of adulterated foods
and ready medicines;
the hospitals with an eye towards business
and the doctor's income;
the homes for the aged
where the aged are forgotten.
All this let us demolish once and for all
with a perfect time bomb;
and of course with the formality of a warning
to those who will wish to stay behind.
But let us wipe out a few hundred million.

PART FOUR
Poems of the 1950's

Sometimes on the subway you see a face.
It transports you. The train moves
as if rattling to heaven, that face,
composed, a sign to be at peace.

Standing on your station platform,
the train moving off,
you firmly believe that someday
you will go with it all the way.

The Painter and Her Subject

My frenzy back and forth has made her sit still.
From color scattered across canvas she traces form,
painfully slow, showing her tongue in exhaustion;
and though from it should come a clown
in mottled red and yellow
and a fairy princess of black eyes and pink smile—
holding a blue scratchy finger to the sky
and a rose dog and somber grey and greenish king,
I believe it is her wishing me well.
                          .

She was busy painting a picture in her room
and I lying on my couch trying to write
I felt lonely and estranged
for all that we had gone through
raising a child. Now
we had different things to perform.

Credo II

Put flowers on the window sill,
give them their water.
Hang pictures on the wall
and let the door to your house stand open.
Let the sun in and let darkness come
when it will.
You will have done no wrong.

The day goes by with its striving
to maintain a way and I remain
cheerful and willing, with the aid
of strength. In the evening
if the way has been found,
each morning it must be discovered anew.
It is night and I gaze out the window
on the vacant street
which too has felt its pressures—
the silence which speaks of achievement.

Daughter so beautiful I cannot believe it
without embarrassment to my sense of fate,
my eyes turned aside, wonder spreading
through me like a dream.
                        Child growing
in my arms, she is renewal of my trust
in goodness and is close to me.

Daughter of my belief, I am the cloud
passing by, illumined by your eyes.
You were born to give me birth again,
with pains and aches, even those
composed of your sleepy cries.

In the street we strolled hand in hand.
I was not a little embarrassed,
looking about at adults with whom
at one time or another I fight
in the subway for space to stand.
Your fingers gripped mine
and I tried to put myself in your place
of absolute innocence and desire.
I think I succeeded because we stood
together in the bakery in line
for cake and bread, with grownups
crowding on us from behind.

The wonder is mine as she counts
the two trees, the two boys and girls.
I am childlike as I listen.
How old am I, I ask,
and the lack of money
to haunt me?
Will I never grow to earn
a living for us both
in ease and plenitude?
Will I always lack the strength
to stand alone? I tighten
my grip on her in my arms
at the open window;
I am growing old.

An Ecology

We drop in the evening like dew
upon the ground and the living
feel it on their faces. Death
soft, moist everywhere upon us,

soon to cover the living
as they drop. This explains
the ocean and the sun.

I stood in the center of a ring of faces.
Beyond them I could see a field of trees.
I moved and the faces moved with me,
I stopped and the faces stopped,
I dropped to the ground
and the ring lowered to my level.
One face opened its lips
and said, We are your fields.

Communion

To say what has to be said here,
one must literally take off one's clothes.
That I will do.
                    Now that I am naked,
you have seen these nipples,
this navel and these thighs
and black beard of my manhood.
All this, you will admit,
is not unexpected. I am
of my own kind
and my heart beats.
I have brothers.

A raven croaking on the perch of my heart,
it was a fledgling when I was born
howling into the night.
                    •
On the shore I crouch
watching death

rise out of the sea
like an island.

Desert People

When they have a place to go to
and when they leave
they walk on sand. In death
their bones are cleaned by sand.
They stake their tents on burial ground
and give their children this
to grow on, as a comfort:
the intimacy of their deaths,
and they lie down with reverence.

Jungle Talk

When monkeys grab each other by the tail
and swing, they pick nuts in a long loop
above the jungle floor; and chew,
spitting the kernels into each other's eyes.
They make a chain to walk from tree to tree,
without touching the lion's ground;
and chatter of their victory,
clambering across each other's back.

At a Dance

Knowing what I know
I wonder what they know
dancing as I have danced
and been unhappy
but made my legs move

quickly without pity
for myself or them,
for knowledge comes
like the theory of light
without an angry cry.
I am ending as the conclusion
to a book. It is being read
and will be laid down
by a reader unknown to me.
My body handles me
and it is a finger
tapping on the earth
for an answer.

The horizon was like an open mouth.
We stepped off the road
to discuss its meaning;
a feeling had grown against
going ahead. We turned
around to retrace our steps.
It was daylight but the way
back took us towards the dusk
deepening around us.
We milled about, touching faces
and bodies, tripped and fell
and trampled on each other;
cried out and ran towards light
again and in the light stood
thinking as dusk moved up on us.
We started to walk again
slowly, into the distance.

And the Wind Comes

The voices of children are the silences
of this world. They shriek and play
and hardly answer the world but grow
and the silence of the questions that we ask
is intensified in their voices.

       They catch
the ball, they run with it and seasons
make them over, with cares transposed
into their arms from shiny spheres;
and seasons pass them and they have shown
another form of earth in time grown still
as questions they have posed for those
who cannot ask the rocks,
and so are caught by questionings.
And children go in silences they have portrayed,
for what is play
but blossoms, and the wind comes.

The faces that judge me,
are they all kindly?
The power they have,
is it all for good?
With no money of my own,
they are the life and death
of my power. My fright
warns me that to look
impersonal is to be taken up
like a stone.

It's this way: the tree has to be pruned
and watered. Do it yourself.
Then turn to the sun.
How else,

when the hired stranger is a lover
too.

.

My self is a watcher
and I sing now.
My self has a world
I call Being Alone.

.

If I can walk farther
than my pain can reach
I'll have entered
a new birth.

At four o'clock I went by
and she was lying there.
At nine, I found her there again
and on my way home finally
past midnight.
Her face wedged between the iron gate
and the stone stair lay pressed flat
against the stone, a drunk and ill
from afternoon till night
in the dress of an ordinary woman.

Communion

Let us be friends, said Walt,
and buildings sprang up
quick as corn and people
were born into them, stock
brokers, admen, lawyers and doctors
and they contended
         among themselves
that they might know
         each other.

Let us be friends, said Walt.
We are one and occasionally two
of which the one is made
and cemeteries were laid out
miles in all directions
to fill the plots with the old
and young, dead of murder, disease,
rape, hatred, heartbreak and insanity
to make way for the new
and the cemeteries spread over the land
their white scab monuments.

Let us be friends, said Walt, and the graves
were opened and coffins laid on top
of one another for lack of space.
It was then the gravediggers slit
their throats, being alone in the world,
not a friend to bury.

The Man Who Attracts Bullets

I'm being shot at in the street.
So far, I have escaped being hit,
feeling the bullets zip by.
I keep walking straight ahead,
making sure not to veer from course
nor duck nor swerve, in case this shooting
is intended simply to scare.

How about this, even seated
in my favorite chair at home
under a lamp with a paper, I feel
the bullets flying by? I sit very still
and imagine what is meant
is a warning to go right on
as I have been going, in a perfectly normal,
calm way.

I have been nicked from time to time
when I have made a wrong move, awkwardly
shifting my feet to cross a mud puddle
or straightening my clothes in the wind.
I'd feel a sting in the arm or ear
and I'd know. When I go to bed
I make sure my head is lying
in the right position for sleep.
I have been shot at in my sleep too,
tossing in a dream. In the morning
I sit up with a splitting headache
or an aching back.

The moral, it seems, is to do what you must
and you will be buried at a ripe age,
blessing your wounds.

The Outlaw

They went after him with a long stick,
jabbing into the hole where he had hid himself
in its dark. If he could be forced out
they would shoot him. The stick dug
into his soft parts but he lay there.
It poked hard and he moved aside.
They would fire into the hole
but that it would seem it was they
who had something to worry about.
The woods darkened and they left.
He came slowly from hiding
and in the silence sat up to lift his voice,
to those beyond the woods about to go to bed,
mournful and prolonged.
For that he was despised.

Life as a Frog

The teacher's calm voice guides him
to lie down in peace at night
among the croaking frogs
of his own backwater. He is ready
to join in the chorus but for the voice
he hears intoning the dry lesson
for the day, with its logic and form.

Frogs are everywhere staring out
of the mouths of his classmates,
out of the teacher's mouth.
His study book lies open before him.

Inevitably a bell clangs an end
to logic and form and he steps
his way out carefully among
the croaking hordes, not to crush
a bulging eye.

I

My life has been a seeking
to identify with pain and suffering
and that is what has made
my friendships strong
and my enmities bitter
and final.

II

I live inside a stone.
What I feel comes to me in waves of sound.
If it is something to hurt
I have it all to myself,
unmoved but hurting;
and if it is something
to make me happy

it is all to myself too,
hurting.
                    For that immobility
and silence people push me aside
with their feet when I stand in the way
and children hurl me into the distance
playfully, children whom I would want
to talk to and influence for the good
by my stoic behavior.
They take it for an invitation
to be playful and skim me
over the surface of a lake
where I sink to the bottom.

Pricing

The grave needed a stone marker.
We picked Flint Rock from New England,
four feet high and three feet wide,
to cover two bodies lying side by side,
my mother and eventually my father.
He stood examining it with us,
his son and two sons-in-law,
in the marble store, and made no comment
other than the weary, grim look
of an old man who has lost his wife,
his only companion, and himself soon to go,
alone now, living among strangers,
though they were his kin.
An old man shuts himself off.
Later after the purchase, as I drove the car,
he tried to say something
to convey his mood and failed,
saying something hackneyed, conscious of it,
and said nothing further, until at home
finally with his daughter he discussed

the price and the stone's color
and its width.

Business

    There is no money in breathing.
    What a shame I can't peddle my breath
    for something else—like what?
    I wish I knew but surely
    besides keeping me alive
    breathing doesn't give enough
    of a return.

    There is tenderness in the voices of two persons
    who live together that tells me they are weary
    of themselves and those familiar ways
    they have devised, as at the request
    to the husband to buy butter—he is immersed
    in chess—he will get up sucking at his pipe
    and with one eye on the retreating board
    reach for his coat and slowly go out the door,
    in hand, placed there by his wife, alert
    to his movements, methodical and fine,
    in hand the money.

Paymaster

    The pay could have been more.
    I felt I was giving myself
    into his hands for judgment.
    Thank you, he said, taking his check.
    Thank me for what, I replied
    silently. I am sending you home,
    belittled in your own eyes.

The Zoo Lion

He gets up from the couch under the closed window
and walks over to the rear wall
where he lies down again upon a sofa
as a change, as a protest.
He has nothing to say, looks out at you,
but then he might turn on his wife
and tear her to pieces. It would
extend the borders of his life
and sex means nothing.
For days he lies alongside the wall.

A Relationship

I shall always love the sea
for it has never spoken harshly
of me. It has meant to drown
or maim me, but never
a harsh word.

Someone I know
whom I feared
now clear and sweet
in his beliefs
teaches me
by his release
to think of joy
and be at peace.
He stood in darkness
for a year
and cried, Stay near!
I did not move,
called to him softly,
I am here.

The Doctor

Entering his office, he looks at his nurse,
hairy, heavy and corseted, nose bulbous,
thick lips that seek the kindness of lipstick.
All of her moves like a ton upon a swinging chain
and as she speaks reminds him of the winds
in the caves of the Pacific shores opening
upon the vacant sea. She speaks, unmarried
to any art or love
and to define herself
moves from desk to his side.

He arrives from a sleepless night of decision
for the ill to whom he has administered his arts
and tricks, all that he has garnered
like fruit with tall reaching or stooping
and patience on one foot, stretching out
for the impossible, to keep alive the dead.

The patient has died. Looking upon the heavy nurse
and the fine bitterness of his longing,
familiar to him as love for which all sacrifice
is just and good and comfortable to one's soul,
for life is us, she approaching him as monolith
to whom life too is given, her tread resounding
on the floor, she makes his human longings
strange to him.

Adonis

I am in love with a pig,
she dances for me
on her hind legs. Good pig,
you must love me
and grateful as I'll be
do not turn savage like a boar,

I might find excuse
to keep you alive,
your tusk buried
in my side.

Communion

In the subway I had the impulse to kill
and sat and stared straight ahead
to avoid the eyes of strangers
who might read my dread
and when finally I had the courage
to shift my gaze from the poster above
I saw to my dismay the eyes of others
turning away.

How to Be Right

Now don't you think you should relax?
Take your son and hit him with an axe;
he's done enough to make it tough for you.
Now do the same unto your wife
who raised your son. Save your life
before it's gone into another coughing fit.
The next may be the last
and what will you have left
behind you as a past but two
who made a life of you,
but if you knock them off instead,
think, although you may end up
electrocuted, you will have had
the last word: it was you
they persecuted.

For those who'll take my place,
I'll leave this peace I devised
for myself: I called upon the quiet air
of the summer and I sat
in the grassy field and examined the daisy.
It had made itself without suffering
to others and had found itself
a place without the use of force
or displacement of others.
Reclining on the grass on one elbow,
I rose up and walked within range
of the guns and the rockets.

In the street, the bug cars scuttle and shoot,
aiming at distance, and you grow wary,
seeing the same carnivori, their backs hunched
to the red light, each morning waiting
and puffing.
          Rest with the trees,
stand with the buildings, struck by lightning,
blasted by peace into wormwood. At dawn,
as you look up from pavement
to the sky, feeling without foothold,
a starry wall is moving steadily back.
What do you say to that, you whining rockets?

There is an apple that must not fall
from its twig;
this one will explode.

Aesthetics II

My poetry was forced on me,
like doodling, waiting
for an interview
that would decide my job.
I grew absorbed in the symbols

and markings. I sat
in the anteroom with other applicants
bored with reading
dated periodicals and books.
I took out my pencil.

Stages

I am somewhere left behind in a dream
that did not end with my awakening
to what I do not own. With music and drums
I awoke, playing me dead rhythms
of mechanical mourning. I reached
for my heart and it was beating
a belonging with the dead
in regular strokes I could not ignore
and did not dare touch for fear
of bursting upon myself. The death
I had was here with me and its sound
was of breathing but there was no
beginning of things. I was breathing
for my own hearing. I was without
a circle to guide me. The way
was towards the distance open
and I was not ending. The drum beat
and the music spared me. I helped
myself with believing in a beginning
back when I had dreamt of an awakening.
Who started the dream, I was whimsical
to ask. Who taught me I was happening?
I had myself and I was dreaming
I am the self and the dream
and who to touch me to hold me
to call me Mine? And who to believe me
and I touch myself with ink
and the image comes forth.

The duck, I tell you, is not resting
inert upon the placid surface, tugged
by a hidden hand or a current. Turning
his head from side to side, observing
the area of his calm, his webbed feet
are making the motions.
He waddles upon shore for food
in the thickets.

Turnings

I

I am thinking my room is green
the sea green the grass
outside my house   I may
have caught a touch of it
The grass and the sea renew themselves
my room remains constant
I am changing in it

.

The odor of an afternoon long ago
comes back in a fragrance of wet grass
I don't know what to do with it
I can't remember when it happened
I know it was intended
as a happy afternoon
I let it pass

.

When I ask who I am I think
of a river with its changing clouds
I think of the clouds and sometimes
of a leaf upon the waves

.

It was raining
the day the world
was born for me
as I stood in a hallway

out of the wet
and stared at the bubbles
bursting
upon pavement

·

Leaves gold red brown black
falling   children walking
to school
their arms embracing books

·

I began as a tree
and now feel the weight
and think height nothing
compared to the burden
of self

·

I am a cover-up for death
my veins my credentials
The figure is made

·

In the morning sun the leaves
fall yellow palegreen and wine
the trees tall as mythical giants
silent
and standing still

II

Wind blow this leaf
brown and skeletal
Leaf be lost
In the woods turn to mold
Leaf is there a death?
Have I lived?

·

That door is closed
you turn around
and walk straight
through the woods
until you reach a pond

turning blue grey white
and sunset red
the crickets
You will want to sleep
calm as the black pond
The stars will have spread
a cover

.

There was a vase that waited for water
There was the film that formed
upon the idle pond
There was the vase drying in the sun

.

It is a silent pond surrounded by silent
woods and shore no animal or man in sight
Here as a child I tossed my pebble
and now my stone
and the ripples fade
my glance as vacant as the smoothness of the pond

.

In a clearing you left behind a house
itself
You remember having closed it
leaving to visit
another place
in a further clearing
only to count the rooms
and the minutes
The door is closed
You remember closing it
and walking off into the woods
your goods upon your back

.

Does the leaf have courage?
Does the tree express a defiance
each stage of its decay?

.

The door opens inward
on silent forms

The doors swings outward
on a trembling leaf
Buildings rise
in light

I was found leaning forward
when I died
my body like a wave
above the shore

My beard rough as the beginning
of things, I'm new today.
You won't find me,
I'll be in the woods
growing a skin
to make friends
with the squirrels, the fox
and the puma; you won't catch me,
I'll be hidden behind their furry selves
and making my own sounds.
Look for me in the trees
or on the mountains,
if you can get away.

This Woman

This woman had her arms around me,
brushing her lips against my face,
making me think the sky had breathed on me
its open spaces. I aroused myself
to embrace her in return—
when she pulled me towards her.
What was my excitement, her every shape
and movement speaking to my body,

calling for my love to wreak upon her,
annihilate her for my own aggrandizement
so that I could know her
in the simple motion of my arm.

She became a burden quickly
when I sought rest. She weighed upon me
in sleep. I was an act of creation
and I lay down to rest, only to feel
her weighing me down. Was there something
I forgot to do to remove her?

And what were her arms doing around my neck
at my desk at work?

The Ice Cream Parlor Romance

After malted, licking his lips, he said,
"Let's separate, honey. I'm bored."
And she, the straw sticking to her lips,
looked up at him from her glass.
They had read somewhere that malted was good
for the nerves and anyway there had always been
this corner candy store to go to.
Now moving away from her drink, she said,
"You louse," in just that tone.
It egged him on, he was sure now.
All he wanted was to make her cry.
"I mean it," he said, and she got up
and walked off haughtily. "How about
a piece of chocolate?" he called after her,
throwing down on the table his tip
and the bill money to follow her out—
she disdained to answer—to work on his triumph,
but not before picking up candy
from the counter, with a wave to the storekeeper
that he would pay later.

Christmas Improvisations

(For Roy Harvey Pearce)

I am the poet of peace,
numbering in my words the harm
that has been, not ignoring
the future. The world can be shattered
by a pin.

•

In my youth I sat and moped
and dreamed up good will
to all and their contentment.
I was discontented,
except in this dreaming
and I decided
that too was real,
I did not have to go out
and slaughter for it.

•

These cannot be words alone to salve my pride;
I have died and I can live again,
close to the ranks of men,
as I sought from the start,
in my single way. Now I see
it needs myself broken apart
and scattered in profusion,
at which I no longer lie in pain,
seeing myself in multiple allusion.

•

Alive, we say, Look, we are alive!
And seek for someone who says Yes,
out of a cloud, or a tree,
or the chirp of a bird,
suddenly intelligible.
We would jump into that cloud,
that tree or catch the bird
to fly us through the eternal air.
Say, we would be happy!

I once had an enemy.
Now he is a person
that I know. He
strikes me
and I sing.
I strike him
and he dances.
Neither wants to die now
unforgiven. It came to us
we were lonely
among the furniture
of self-esteem.

The baker eats cake with his problems:
the scalding heat, the hot handle
to the dough plate and the constant
tickling dusty flour. His brows
and hair white like a worried old man's.
He chews his own bread,
patting his stomach.

Note on Turgenev

There is no settling down anywhere;
in the country we hear the hunter's gunfire;
the rabbit scoots under our porch
and the hunter approaches.

My arms raised above my head,
palms placed flat against the wall,
I am waiting for it to turn inwards
like a door. Behind me is a silent drop.

I sleep through the night and each morning
expect to find an opening, at least a crack
through which to see what lies beyond,
to make me persevere. By noon I despair
and by evening am weary unto death.
But having found myself here,
I expect there must be reason,
given my hopes and fears.

Love me love my bombs
each prays in the din.
None hears himself addressed,
waiting for silence
that a bomb could leave
and a voice calling,
Love me love my bombs.
And the shocked mountains
roll their rocks
into the valley.

Let the bombs hang in air a moment
while we adjust to their coming,
making ourselves secure in our will
to die as we are, unrepentant
but forgiving, since we cannot
go on breathing except as we are.
Therefore to be remembered
as we were by the bone pickers
who know the taste of flesh.

Reading at Night

What have I learned that can keep me
from the simple fact of my dying?
None of the ideas I read stay
with me for long. I find the dark
closed in about me as I close
the book and I hurry to open it
again to let its light shine
on my face.

from The Gentle Weight Lifter *(1955)*

To Rose Graubart and Milton Hindus

Lives II

At Colonnus Oedipus complained,
Antigone attended him. He thought
the sun too hot, she shielded him;
his enemies too strong, she fought
for him; his life bitter, she soothed him
and bathed his blinded eyes.
And when he left, forced by decree,
she went with him, her arm supporting him;
and when he lay at the end of his strength,
stretched out upon the forest floor,
his head pillowed in her lap,
his arms at his sides trembling,
he thought surely some cover
could be found for him.

The Men Sang

Nicias warned them: in Sicily stood ruin;
in no country were they wanted,
in their own they were besieged.
What could Athenians seek to gain?
And Athens roared back, Traitor!
And Alcibiades got secretly together
his compatriots to desecrate the state,
to hasten their rupture with the past—of freedom
and forebearance; Nicias made to take command
of all forces, challenged to. Gold
glittered in their eyes, from Syracuse.
And against every impulse, sick with grief,
foreboding each step, Nicias set sail;
and the men sang, and rowed
as never before.

from The Gentle Weight Lifter *(1955)* 8 9

The Stranger

That face grown hair, flat-lipped,
ears like pointed spears, tufts shoot from them—
this face human by virtue of our fright.
What stirs in us? This flat mouth talks:
Have mercy, I am of the species . . .
We shoot him on sight, he dies for us,
lies prone in our brain a terror; not human,
no, never, we with tactile skin. Kill, for God's
    sake.
Do not listen to the monster that will persuade us
in our accents. Fire into its throat, its magic,
its evil, its death of the human. Who was the
    woman
bore it? Think it woman and die shuddering,
but kill! And he conquers, rises from the dead
around him, freed by their deaths; and mourns,
bewailing his fate to be alone, to eat and sleep
    alone,
to adventure alone: cry of the human;
he mourns his dead and his fate, beating his chest.
And they rise, now that they are done for,
now that there is nothing to lose they take him
to their breasts; they accept, weeping.

The Faithful One

Praying, he moves among those holding knives.
He has been cut and does not mind now.
The air is noisy, the crowds large.
He moves or is pushed, no thrust
directly aimed at him. Swaying
or knocked aside, he feels no pain,
no weakening from loss of blood.
Who sees him turns astonished,
and turns quickly back to his blade.

Is there one who from mere pleasure
will thrust him dead?
He walks, faithful.

The Pardon of Cain

Who did you kill that you thought would make
     life simpler
by dying? Your hands are trembling, your rage
is eating at you. Look at your face, pale
and haggard; at your eyes, insane.
He haunts you as the one with whom life was
     well enough,
there being life in him to instruct you. Torment
was your knowledge so that, subsiding beneath discipline,
shy calm and its joy come in place.
This you forgot as you suffered, and lashed out
and saw him die, to leave you alone with the
     murder,
and your two fists of wrong;
and because your face now is death's own,
in his absence; because of this agony
of the uselessness of death to the living, such is
     your joy
in this knowledge now that you may live again.

c. 1949

The Sphinx
(On holidays the Egyptians with their children play an obstacle-racing
game on these stones.)

They had stood in the sun and piled up these
     stones
to tell us life was that hard and that high and
     wide

from The Gentle Weight Lifter *(1955)* 9 1

and filled with so many tall steps that needed our
    hands
and legs and full strength to rise upon; and now
descendants, lives no grander, no gayer, no easier
by one less stone—who still drink from sandy wells,
they do not deny it—clamber upon them
with their children on a picnic spree.

What have you taught them
but the exercise of their wills,
to make a jest of their hardships?

They shall ascend, each child and his parent,
to wisdom's face and mount the body
as on a flying lion for the love of it
that one moment permits before the next;
and then, not to fall to tears and helpless rage,
descend racing in a game.

In Ancient Times

And they took Abu and stoked the fire with him,
and then Azu, after Abu was consumed,
to keep the blaze high. It was a night
of wild animals, a fire was needed to ward them
    off.
Abu by his own choice was killed for fuel
and then Azu to keep the others safe;
and so on down the line, one by one,
until morning. Men, women and children
who would not die in this manner
were forced to by their own hand,
for the sake of the others,
after a long talk.

And in the morning
the great band arose from around the dead ash

and moved on to new grounds and new possibilities;
and in the afternoon as always
when they were starved paired off
and killed each other for their food.
There was nothing to eat over the whole wide plain
of their wandering, and nothing to work with
to turn the soil—like lead, anyhow.
They had come by a blind route from orchards
and fields in their wandering to this
forsakenness, over which the lions howled
for the flesh that crawled by.

Mystique

No man has seen the third hand
that stems from the center,
near the heart. Let either
the right or the left prepare
a dish for the mouth,
or a thing to give,
and the third hand deftly
and unseen will change the object
of our hunger or of our giving.

Bothering Me at Last

Where is my mother?
Has she gone to the store for food,
or is she in the cellar shoveling coal
into the furnace to keep the house warm?
Or is she on her knees scrubbing the floor?
I thought I saw her in bed
holding a hand to her heart, her mouth open.
"I can't breathe, son. Take me to a hospital."
I looked for her in the cellar.

from The Gentle Weight Lifter *(1955)* 93

I looked for her in bed, and found her in her
          coffin,
      bothering me at last.

Promenade

      His head split in four parts,
      he walks down the street—pleasant
      with shady trees and a sun softened
      by leaves touching it. He walks,
      a revolving turret for a head,
      from each slit of which he looks guardedly:
      the enemy approaches or he approaches
      the enemy. At any moment the chatter of differences
      will break out; the four parts of his skull
      revolve slowly, seeking the time.

      In there they do not know of each other,
      sealed off by steel walls. They are safer
      together, singly and apart;
      while overhead, ignored in the walk,
      are the leaves, touching each other and the sun.

The Hunter

      While birds nest, I carry a gun.
      To study them in their mating season
      is my wish, but I carry a gun that goes off
      at sudden intervals. In the tone of my voice,
      in this dilemma, I believe I am the gun:
      a phrase shot out that makes those who hear it
      wince. I only have heard the report and recoil
      mechanically, tense to see birds in their mating.

I must walk around as a gun, people step aside
at a glance. Is my expression the hair trigger
they dare not come near? I must stand like a
            gun.
In any direction I turn they vanish from my view.
Buildings, only buildings dare stand. I could blast
them with my eyes, but turn away. On cold days
I need their comfort to walk into.

Birds in their mating season, I see them in streets,
too, pecking at stones. How many such have vanished
in my look? I am a menace to myself even
in the mirror, each hole in my face
of deadly caliber. All at once I fire
and vanish, even as a gun, and become nothing—
once more human.

News Report

At two A.M. a thing, jumping out of a manhole,
the cover flying, raced down the street,
emitting wild shrieks of merriment and lust.
Women on their way from work, chorus girls
or actresses, were accosted with huge leers
and made to run; all either brought down
from behind by its flying weight, whereat
it attacked blindly, or leaping ahead,
made them stop and lie down.

Each, hysterical, has described it in her way,
one giving the shaggy fur, the next the shank bone
of a beast, and a third its nature
from which, as it seemed, pus dribbled,
when she saw no more—
                        all taking place
unnoticed until the first report, hours later
when consciousness was regained, and each

from diverse parts of the city has a telltale
sign, the red teeth marks sunk into the thigh
and the smell of a goat clinging tenaciously
through perfume and a bath.

Consolation

I think that when the yellow pillow
is thrown against the blue wall
God is in the room, for I know
there can be no ultimate evil—
when as an argument ensues
yellow is shown in glowing contrast
to deep blue.

The Painter

When she sees parrots and princesses they are there,
her tongue tip protruding from between clenched
teeth.
Eyes do not leave the canvas, and when she breaks
off
it is to remove herself. She will walk safely
through the streets, wide-eyed, smiling and talking
and even eating; but then, awakened, rested, her
face
clouding, the line of her lips straightening,
she goes to her brushes, and she lives.

In the gay colors given him, the parrot envies
her.
How, head cocked to a side, he seems to ask,
has she learnt about him, she who is human?
The princess in the gesture painted for her waves:
be one like me, since you know me so well,

loving finery and its ceremony. But how,
the still gesture implies, is paint become familiar
with my thoughts, you who are distant from me,
your smeared smock, your hairband.

With painting, these questions are answered,
the colors to blend yet more subtly and somber,
as love will impose upon dreams, their realness
tested. The parrot growing more harsh-looking,
being made to live, its beak hoarse with fruit lust
grows durable; and gay as the princess
was at the start, now she must always be gay,
and the colors and the light gesture of greeting
have turned inward, so that joy is its memorial.

These are not dreams, and the brush stroke is the
        agent.
At the hour of appropriate exhaustion, leaving the
        field
of canvas, she ravens on the transient bread and
        cheese,
this hunger beyond herself. Done with this passage
of things, sleep calls, of this other world.
In obedience she lies down. Now fretted in sleep,
finds herself involved in the tinder of arms,
legs and brushwood hair, husband lover thrown to
        her
by the power beyond herself, with the largeness
of the world. Still she sleeps, her eyes wide,
strength in her arms, resting. This is the world
she had been ordered to, exhaustion its herald;
and as much as can be found of it she accepts
and believes, for the fleeting and soon gone
makes of an instant a place too.

Gulls

They thread the air
and sew up the uneven parts
into a pattern to which wings
lend authority.
                    They settle
upon waves, compact upon motion;
and rise, to assert motion.

It is with evening,
their wings covered by darkness
suffusing space, that they cry;
and have a sounding board, the waves,
to measure space.

                                        c. 1940

Poem

A view of the mountain from the valley floor,
he who sees it understands,
and he who must read of it brings himself.
I cannot put him into words,
though his eyes move my thoughts to live.
I write of him
so that he may know my mountain.

Escape

There was a man in me who bit his lips
and talked bitterly, and I spoke up for him
at the known councils and I said as much
to everyone. They were prepared
and showed me each the dangers they had mapped.
Would I be risky, as my share?
Would I go everywhere?

And I made quick answer, saying yes,
and stillness waited on me
in the meaning I professed,
and I ran and ran. This was the danger
each found to my plan;
and bitter-lipped I stood with my inside man,
until I breathed his air,
and I ran from there.

Dedication
(For L. C. Woodman)

To one who clambered upon a white horse
one rainy night, and galloped off under lightning,
a warning to the world in bold handwriting
in his pocket, a love letter to the wife
of another man in another pocket.

The night transformed itself into a show
of stars, and under this canopy, he dismounted
to find peace. Plucked grass, ate earth,
sang to the trees, and lay with stones,
but was dissatisfied. Hell was his biggest lack.
He missed the murders, screams of lunatics,
he missed music such as he understood,
the last blood-garbled speech of the slain.
Mounted and rode off again,
into the rocky sea that shone
under the moon like a dirt road.

Needless to say, his head was found floating
above the waves, still with its lips formed
in a song of the dead.

from The Gentle Weight Lifter *(1955)* 99

Singers of Provence

Was it beauty for one's head
to be hoisted upon a petard,
or to be run through with the sword,
or to be strung up by the wrists
for some slight against your king,
singers of Provence? You made music
to cover your guilt, you were all scared;
and you sang to bring on the ecstasy of lies;
while we with the door wide open
on the scene of the crime face the day
clearly with these words: We were here
and we witnessed the deaths and drownings,
the deeds too dark for words;
they would rumble in the belly meaninglessly,
but we speak our minds and the song sticks.
The people sing it, the singer believes it,
The air springs with a new song.

The High Diver

The sea will receive him as a guest
and distance accordingly shrink
to his leap. There is danger in drawing back;
the body, without one's pride, a mere pittance,
without honor. It is this quality,
not to be conceived of by the sea or high cliff
but innate in them that shall force them
from their purpose, to kill him.
He takes off his clothes for his return.
It shall not be without honor nor without witness.
He leaps and the air leaps with him
to carry him down at his speed. The fish
inhabiting the area expect him or someone like him;
their mouths open and close.

A Guided Tour Through the Zoo

Ladies and gentlemen,
these are pygmies, fated to live
in small perspective; children
of their shrunk parents, who
because of stubborn pride fed
on small seeds and herbs, scrabbled
together with hooded eyes; and so
were grown to such likeness; but
in turn had been shut in by their parents
in caves to be told night was day;
for their parents' parents were fledged
on the precipice from which they fled
to these caves, and so on, giving us
this tribe before us.
                    The story is sad,
for they remember by lost meanings
of words that they were of Hercules,
who could move earth for fleas to rest
easy, or sheep to roll softly downhill.
They were men, so called, in their unworded
language, which, when the sun grows brutal
with them as with rocks, they cry
remembrance in these open fields,
their homes under the short grass.
Ladies and gentlemen, let us move on
now to the cage of wild wolves.

Dilemma

Whatever we do, whether we light
strangers' cigarettes—it may turn out
to be a detective wanting to know who is free
with a light on a lonely street nights—
or whether we turn away and get a knife
planted between our shoulders for our discourtesy;
whatever we do—whether we marry for love

from The Gentle Weight Lifter *(1955)*   101

and wake up to find love is a task,
or whether for convenience to find love
must be won over, or we are desperate—
whatever we do; save by dying,
and there too we are caught,
by being planted too close to our parents.

The Dancer

It wasn't to shake her body that she danced
nor to make eyes either, but to spell
in one motion cat, dog, pig and waterfall,
by a flip of the hip or wrist or twist
of the torso—goat, lamb, wind or lover.
She rolled upon the floor and bit her nails,
leaped up and grabbed the air, swung her head
    low
between her knees and walked that way,
arms dropping between her outspread legs:
an old man, an elephant and stalking tiger;
or just plain being tired of it all.

Flat upon her back, she was the world
before Columbus' time, here and there
a shape thrown outwards, stomach breathing,
breasts sloping down from the world's edge.
With morning at the window and a drink,
she stretches forward, as exercise,
to touch toes: the world coming together
for one more show.

Man's Posture

There are many forms of love, but none
that can deny it; and so there is tenderness

and waiting in each, unless out of a fear
they are estranged. Then love grows rounded
like a ball, with that quality, rebounding,
struck: itself, as love should not be.
It is a catacomb to be entered into,
under pressure expanding: a dwelling
for the disinherited and despised
awaiting torture.
                Be torn by lions of the day,
love rends us. Or we must walk among our fellow
    men,
at peace in our deaths, not knowing
the difference between a flower and a spittoon,
between sitting and walking, running and racing,
and the panting breath at the far end
of the field where nothing awaits us
but a fence over which the ash heap lies:
dumping grounds that someday shall become
new racing fields. In our panted breath
we shall expend ourselves, seeking no cause
or climax: golden trophies or fair kisses,
too tired, too happy in our weariness:
loss of the heavy part of us, run
to be rid of it: love forcing us, living us,
wearing us. Finally, when we are useless
to other needs, tearing us to pieces by lions
before the crowd.
                For love is when we are racing,
expressed in tenderness and waiting.
Wait always. Waiting we are racing.
And tenderness is our posture, not crouched,
not forward, nor leaning backwards but upright
like a man in which love can recognize itself.
                          c. 1943

Oedipus Reformed

I will not kill my father,
he must die of admiration.
I will not lay a hand on him,
I will not curse or nag
or make him to explode angrily
so that his mind bursts.
Here is myself realized,
I have everything I ever dreamt,
and I shall attend his funeral,
mourning my lost heart;
for with him goes my impulse.
And then I will raise him in my eyes,
we will be one.
My wife will play my mother
and be kind.

The Gentle Weight Lifter

Every man to his kind of welcome in the world,
some by lifting cement barrels, laboring.
He looks so stupid doing it, we say.
Why not a soft job, pushing a pencil
or racketeering, the numbers game?
As the pattern is rigged, he must
get love and honor by lifting barrels.

It would be good to see a change,
but after barrels he cannot fool with intangibles.
He could with his muscular arm sweep them aside
and snarl the tiny lines
by which he can distinguish love.

He is fixed in his form,
save a hand reach from outside
to pick him up bodily and place him,

still making the movements that insure his love,
amidst wonders not yet arrived.

The Fisherwoman

> She took from her basket four fishes
> and carved each into four slices
> and scaled them with her long knife,
> this fisherwoman, and wrapped them;
> and took four more and worked
> in this rhythm through the day,
> each action ending on a package
> of old newspapers; and when it came
> to close, dark coming upon the streets,
> she had done one thing, she felt, well,
> making one complete day.

Lunchtime

> None said anything startling from the rest;
> each held her coffee cup in her own way,
> and one twanged, another whined and a third
> shot out her phrases like a rear exhaust;
> yet each stood for the same things:
> the clothes in their conversation,
> the food they ate and the men they could not
> catch up with. They were not saying more
> than could be said in a crowd, they made this
> their unity, as the thinking of one person;
> and getting up to go, lunch over
> by the clock, each pulled out her own chair
> from underneath her.

Office Party

The hips go circling in the slow suggestive manner
of the loving. This is wild music they hear:
the cymbals whine, the trumpet jitters
the trumpet player, his fingers panicked
over the keys; and the drum rolls long
pounding waves. This is wild music
after five, and the husband home
tossing a paper in his chair. Shove
aside the filing cabinets, get the pencils
out of sight and rub off the carbon stain
from your fingers. Cut loose!
The jazzmen pouring it on get fifty
dollars for the night. How they play
for their money!

I Want

I'll tell him I want to be paid immediately.
I'll sue him, I'll tear down his place,
I'll throw a fit, I'll show him whether
he can make me miserable.
I want things perfect.
I want to know I can expect a check
tomorrow morning at nine o'clock
exactly, with the mailman,
and if he doesn't bring it
I'll know that he too has done it
on purpose. He too knows
I have a family and a business
that are going to be made miserable by me.
At home I'll snarl and in the office
nobody will talk to me,
I'll talk to nobody,
and over the phone I'll whine
about money. Is that nice?

And what will people think of me?
It'll be some world,
a horrible one already,
the way I'm upset and with nothing to do
but rave, rave, rave.
I want my check!

The Salesman

What a busy man I was, I had first to step into
    one place
to confirm a price, and then on to the next to
    fix a date
and in that same building visit a third. There was
    even more
in those two hours but I hurried with legs stretched
    out
ahead of me like a horse and when through, exhausted,
plopped into a seat in a courtroom near my last
    errand
where the listening was free, and heard three men
condemned to prison for larceny, felony and assault
respectively, and each one take it calmly
and each as normal as myself in looks;
they stood quiet before the judge;
and then two women for assault upon their neighbors—
given each three months. But only one difference
did I note: I wore a business suit—
and I did think they spoke incorrectly
or at least with no feeling. In effect
they said nothing before the judge,
and I sitting there noticing the courtroom crowded
with such cases, badged men strolling among them
to keep order, and men along the walls to overlook
the room, and hour after hour going by and no
    letup,
the court crowded as ever; they were, literally,

being brought in off the streets. I left
and went into traffic.

Sales Talk

Better than to kill each other off
with our extra energy is to run after the bus,
though another be right behind. To run
and to explain to ourselves we have no time
to waste, when it is time that hangs
dangerously on our hands, so that the faster
we run the quicker the breezes rushing by
take time away.
          For comfort we must work
this way, because in the end we find
fume-filled streets and murder headlines:
one out of insanity breaks loose:
he could not make that extra effort
to keep connected with us. Loneliness
like a wheeling condor was attracted
to the particle that had strayed apart.
The brief case we carry, the pressed trousers,
the knotted tie under a white collar add up
to unity and morale.

The Business Life

When someone hangs up, having said
to you, "Don't come around again,"
and you have never heard the phone
banged down with such violence
nor the voice vibrate with such venom,
pick up your receiver gently and dial
again, get the same reply; and dial
again, until he threatens. You will

then get used to it, be sick only
instead of shocked. You will live,
and have a pattern to go by, familiar
to your ear, your senses and your dignity.

In Place of Love

In place of love we must have money:
fifteen thousand for her house
the woman requires, not a penny less—
standing fine-lipped in her parlor.
Grey-haired, though young in the hips
and eyes. A little smile, perhaps
a return motion of the hips,
would bring the price closer to love.

From male to male she looks
for whom to trust in the bargaining,
the son or the father—here to buy.
And the house empty, save for a sister
her own greying age, dishwashing
in the kitchen. A man's voice, laughing
but gentle, and the clatter stops;
a chalk face peeks past the door:
a little love. The parlor couch torn
in the middle shows no love.
She who is fine-lipped looks hastily
at the tear, and stammers about "no time,"
the house in disrepair. No doubt,
and the eyes blue and direct explain
what is missing.
            With tea between her
and the guests, her own laughter warmed
from the tension of her lips, the price too
has begun to ease: a wavering
between thirteen and fourteen.
Her arm draped over the couch,

sat in gracefully, the hand begins to caress
the cloth absentmindedly.

The Reward

They who love me stand in my way
of being taken care of and fondled;
they call on me for help.
I am afraid, after all, that to scream
and rant will be my downfall.
They will see me coming and run,
and I will die of loneliness;
and so you see me either accompanying my wife
on her walks or in my aged father's business,
and no one would know that I am impatient,
least of all my friends who come to me
with their thoughts. I embrace them,
shielding myself with their presence.

The Preparation

And how I sat and gave a wall my love
and study, propped upon a bed,
and how I was happy to have in front of me
a wall. In this way my mind was free.
And how I then took its findings
to find me those in whom I observed
the same degree, that we were not
so much alike as happy with one another.
We were not setting devices to deceive,
for the wall stopped me.
Those I found were like walls to me
in reflecting my own lack of adornment,
for I had above their heads
the deepening sky.

Moving Picture

When two take gas
by mutual consent
and the cops come in
when the walls are broken down
and the doctor pays respects
by closing the books
and the neighbors stand about
sniffing and afraid
and the papers run a brief
under a whiskey ad
and the news is read
eating ice cream or a fruit
and the paper is used
to wrap peelings
and the garbage man
dumps the barrel
into the truck
and the paper flares
in the furnace and sinks back
charred and is scooped up
for mud flats and pressed down
by steam rollers for hard ground
and a house on it
for two to enter.

Elegy

I must wait for a stranger to knock on my door.
For one month I have lain on my couch waiting
for a friendly knock. Why has there been none?
Why outside is the sound always of traffic,
the high-pitched impersonal hard rubber?
The sunlight has been a composition,
it poses for me like a cold model.
My presence here has begun to feel like an intrusion.

from The Gentle Weight Lifter *(1955)*   111

What have I stirred up to anger that refuses
to talk to me or even to knock? What in my
     behavior
has been offensive, though I recall only
my good humor? When did I last speak to someone?
I cannot recall even, and may be making up
to salvage my pride this being good-natured,
for it is so distant that its reality is like an echo
that I can suspect only as a distortion of my mind.
I shall wait for a stranger,
and if in fact I have not been good to my friends
I will be so now to a stranger.

An Illusion

She was saying mad things,
like To hell with the world!
Love is all you need! Go on
and get it! What are you
waiting for! And she walked,
more like shuffled up the street,
her eyes fixed in the distance.
She would not divert them
for a moment. People stepped
self-consciously out of the way.
Straight up stood her hair, wild.

What are you waiting for, snarled
from her lips; it seemed directed
really to herself, to someone inside
with whom she fought. The shredded hem
of her dress rustled around her.

The Debate

This man brings me stones
out of the ground. These
are eggs, he says, of the Jurassic
age, hardened. They may
be looked upon as eggs.
And taking them in awe
I drop them. They bounce,
one strikes me on the toe,
I wince. They are eggs,
he repeats calmly.
They are stone, I shout.
Stone, stone! They were eggs
in their day and bruise me now.
They are eggs, ossified,
he amends calmly.
And I will not let you
fry them for breakfast,
I answer sweetly,
because they are stone.

At the Museum

I see that the stillness of a statue
is the first order of beauty,
so that I may be there
though in its gesture it would be
elsewhere. With this statue
I share a life and yet can pity it
for being stone, pleased too
that stone has shape; and I say,
being held, I was not wrong
to stay.

The American and Lend-Lease

And they come begging for money
with scorn, proud of their past
where money had no part. They had fought
battles and died brave, dedicated
to love or to philosophy. He must bow
his head in deference and give.

They have not asked him how his wealth
was made, in what self-doubt and aspiration,
emptiness there. To make something solid
out of air, the thick woods and rough hills
that repelled him. He had dug, cursing
and brawling to keep up his grit,
and grew coarse to keep the strength strong;
for he had inherited a vast emptiness
of wild animals and grass of which
he could not eat steadily without turning.

Before him stood this dim past,
a ghost driving him, terrified
by its glory, to escape and make a present
equal to it and unafraid.
He has it in his wealth.

A hill has broken down in me,
and God stands on my level now.
Between the two of us a look will pass,
and God embarrassed at events
looking at me long and clear.

The Aged Poet

His belly projects, as if to say,
This now takes precedence,
I have thought up to the start of death.
While I live it must be with the aid of my body.
His humor is passing and light,
with the regimen of age,
and his form hardly matters
but that it brings a voice, detached,
for he retains a victory in his posture,
of knowledge and sharing.

For All Friends

Talking together, we advance from loneliness
to where words fall off into space
and send up no echo. Looking down
for instruction, we gaze into the crease
and fold of each other's face.
We are falling, our flesh aged
by life's upward force.
Our words are buried in the falling air.
Deep in the ground,
we will be one with our words,
for earth too falls towards eternity.

from Say Pardon *(1961)*

To W. C. Williams and Rose Graubart

SECTION ONE

How Come?

I'm in New York covered by a layer of soap foam.
The air is dense from the top of skyscrapers
to the sidewalk in every street, avenue
and alley, as far as Babylon on the East,
Dobbs Ferry on the North, Coney Island
on the South and stretching far over
the Atlantic Ocean. I wade
through, breathing by pushing
foam aside. The going is slow,
with just a clearing ahead
by swinging my arms. Others are groping
from all sides, too. We keep moving.
Everything else has happened here
and we've survived: snow storms,
traffic tieups, train breakdowns, bursting
water mains; and now I am writing
with a lump of charcoal stuck between my toes,
switching it from one foot to the other—
this monkey trick learned visiting
with my children at the zoo of a Sunday.
But soap foam filling the air,
the bitter, fatty smell of it . . . How come?
My portable says it extends to San Francisco!
Listen to this, and down to the Mexican border
and as far north as Canada. All the prairies,
the Rocky Mountains, the Great Lakes, Chicago,
the Pacific Coast. No advertising stunt
could do this. The soap has welled out of the ground,
says the portable suddenly. The scientists report
the soil saturated. And now what?
We'll have to start climbing for air,
a crowd forming around the Empire State Building
says the portable. God help the many
who will die of soap foam.

from Say Pardon *(1961)* 119

The News Photo

> This idiot had suffered his own faults,
> but since it was this country
> and he had done a thing beyond himself,
> by the axe, and since it was an act
> that could be called public,
> in the interest of the public to be known,
> he was to be shown in this act,
> in its way instructive: they had been his parents
> and he had tried not to,
> shouting at them to beware, as they slept;
> he had wept, and since in this manner
> he had cleansed himself,
> he could grin for his picture.

Doctor

> The patient cries, Give me back feeling.
> And the doctor studies the books:
> what injection is suitable for hysterics,
> syndrome for insecurity, hallucination?
> The patient cries, I have been disinherited.
> The doctor studies the latest bulletins
> of the Psychiatric Institute and advises
> one warm bath given at the moment of panic.
> Afterwards inject a barbiturate. At this
> the patient rises up from bed and slugs
> the doctor and puts him unconscious to bed;
> and himself reads the book through the night
> avidly without pause.

Obsolete

> I'm going to drive up
> to the gate and tell him

to take the knock out
of the motor and the bump
out of the spring
and straighten the bent-in side,
repaint the body
and put in new upholstery.
I'll pay him a fair price.
I've sat behind this wheel
ten years. I don't need
a new car, I just need
repairs. This fellow
will blow up, he'll go mad,
he'll want to beat me,
his eyes bloodshot, his voice
thick to know if I'm a wise guy,
with him standing
in front of his new cars
and if he pulls me out
and beats me, I'll know
damn well he's admitting
he can't make me obsolete.

Side by Side

What does it mean to be mature?
We have got to take hold of the fellow
we work with and whom we trust to be true
to us in a crisis and say to him,
gripping him by the shirt front
near the throat, our face thrust into his:
snarl at him, "Now look here, I see clear
through you, playing me for a sucker
by being nice to me. You want to get away
with something without paying for it.
I am not going to let you, see?
I am not going to be taken advantage of,
and when I get the chance to do what I want

I shall do it with much more ruthlessness
than you and not be tied up in feelings.
After that I shall be friends with you,
once I have what I want from you."
This being maturity, I turn to him
as we sit side by side working
and say aloud so that it may be heard
all over, "Give me a cigarette, will you,
I'm all out of them."

Shined Shoes

Get a shine. Who knows, it might lead to money.
Somebody seeing you well groomed, thinking
this man has no real need, will approach
and say, I have money for you.
At this point, overcome by pride
I will respond, I have plenty of my own,
at which he will know, since there is no end
to the need, that like so many with shined shoes,
I live on a budget.

Mr. Mammon I

It was no use their pleading with me
to whom they came for pay Fridays.
I demanded loyalty, efficiency,
promptness and no problem about it.
I would raise my voice too in anger
or sarcasm and I would see white
come into their faces. At these moments
one would walk out the door
and not return. I'd have to mail
the final check. The others
would go about their work dazed-looking.

I'd be sorry but I'd be practical too,
entering my office and shutting the door
behind me. I was no dream of human perfection,
nor did I intend that in business.
Miserable as they were the most part of the week,
holidays would have them pray for perfect mercy,
which left me to feel an outsider,
and I did not pray, standing in Our Lord's presence
for judgment, as I felt myself
each day of the week.

Mr. Mammon II

In business my ideal is to get up
to adjust a screw or a bill
or a customer's complaint,
taking in all about ten minutes;
then to retire hands in pockets
to my office and stand looking
out the window at traffic
and to hear the machines go
inside the shop and to feel
I am lending my presence.
I would have a relationship to God
to think about. I would feel
His presence, along with unease
at my freedom, and I would imagine
this condition something to bear
gracefully, requiring just this
idleness. And I would remove
my hands from my pockets
and return to the shop
and stroll its length and width,
looking over my machines and help,
in pity and humiliation.
I would know what it means
to betray, to invite betrayal.

from Say Pardon *(1961)* 123

And I would reply, Oh Lord,
why did you give me this desire
for freedom, if not to feel
myself in your presence?

The Errand Boy I

To get quicker through the day
and to bring on night as a blessing,
to lie down in a sleep that is a dream
of completion, he takes up his package
from the floor—he has been ordered
to do so, heavy as it is, his knees weakening
as he walks, one would never know
by his long stride—and carries it
to the other end of the room.

The Errand Boy II

It was the way he went to pick up the carton
fallen to the gutter from his handtruck,
his arms outstretched, his body stooping
to the ground. I wondered at the smile,
weary and amused and so gentle withal,
as if this was what he had expected,
not for the first time and not
for the last time either.

The Manager

I want no balking, no hesitation
as to my meaning, not even
at the slightest pressure

of my thumb, and I will not feel
miserable about it. I will have nothing
rub me the wrong way, I will have everything
my way and the result will be
that I will not know which way
is which, with everything giving in
at a look; and think,
I'll not have anger to bear
any longer, I'll be happy dead.

The Paper Cutter

He slides the cut paper out
from under the raised knife.
His face does not lose interest.
"And now I go to my night job,"
he says cheerfully at five,
wiping his hands upon a rag.
He has stood all day in one spot,
pressing first the left
and then the right button.
"And what are you going to do
with all that money?" I ask.
His shoulders stick out bony.
"I will buy a house
and then I will lie down in it
and not get up all day," he laughs.

The Dream

Someone approaches to say his life is ruined
and to fall down at your feet
and pound his head upon the sidewalk.
Blood spreads in a puddle.
And you, in a weak voice, plead

with those nearby for help;
your life takes on his desperation.
He keeps pounding his head.
It is you who are fated;
and you fall down beside him.
It is then you are awakened,
the body gone, the blood washed from the ground,
the stores lit up with their goods.

The Transcendentalist Walking Through Skid Row

He is in the secret
though he could not tell you
for money or for truth its substance,
which is the way of a man
who can tell himself his good fortune
and his desires were vague.
He allows himself neither shame nor terror,
and he is gone to his business
off the street of sprawled men
before they can sit up to talk to him.
He will be justified in his preoccupation.
He presumes much.
It is a happy thought.

Night People

See them with their backs
to the sun, studying their shadows
long and dark, and none thinks
to turn around. It will be night
and they will begin to move
among themselves silently,
touching each other for signposts.
No one will speak

and no arm be raised
in a gesture, as they vanish.

Each Night

I see a flat hat upon the river;
beneath it, I imagine, my cousin,
face rigid with thought, eyes closed
the better to see; and still, still
as a monument for the sound.

He was an artist, faces caught
within a frame by shadow; desiring light
only, they gazed fixedly out.
     •   •   •   •   •
In your tenement, soiled shades
of the poor, your brush lies idle,
while from the rain-blotched wall
hangs the burlesque of a millionaire.
I could not believe in it, Al;
each stroke deliberately crude but caricatured
your sadness: your mother's breasts and belly
bleary and drawn: her voice instructing you
in the sounds of the world—full of complaint;
your father's reply rough, and dead
in its decisiveness. He could not be budged,
curt as the limits he had set.
All this was your legitimate complaint.

Float away from me, my kin; my grief
and sinking sigh the waves and the trough
carrying you, touching and withdrawing
and touching once more to find you dead.
     •   •   •   •   •
But each night, crossing the bridge from work,
I look for you, tiny light refractions
from my train dot and dash signals upon the waves,

"Come out." See, each morning I ride willingly,
and at night compose poems to tiredness
and disillusion, and to hope pinnacled
upon receding towers. I too emerged
from a hardening womb: choked arteries,
stalled vehicles belching frustration,
where bums lie sprawled, toxic with fumes—
and children white with wanting
upon the narrow causeways. My parents
were the city and its complaint of brakes
and horns. For food I sucked at exhaust pipes,
and heard overhead rumbling motor of argument,
playing in my mother's lap, the gutter.
Now grown, drunk and staggering from my repast,
I travel between home and hell, always
with a pencil, to punch holes for air
when breathing becomes difficult.

Each night, crossing the bridge, train lights
appeal to you, Take back your brush,
Oh reach for it from the river.

c. 1940

Say Pardon

Say pardon to a bum,
brushing past him.
He could lean back
and spit
and you would have to wipe it off.
How would you explain
that you have insulted
this man's identity,
of his own choosing;
and others could only scratch
their heads and advise you
to move on

and be quiet.
Say pardon
and follow your own will
in the open spaces ahead.

My Pity

This locked man,
a springer of death upon himself,
shut face. His look is killing,
I am deprived of my pity.
There is motion,
he has crossed a leg,
his agony embodied.
I know, for I withdraw myself
from its sight,
my pity back again.

The Complex

My father's madness is to own himself,
for what he gives is taken. He is
a single son of God. He is mad
to know the loves he owns are for his keeping,
so if he does not love he is without himself,
for God has said, Of love you are a man.
You are yourself, apart from me.
And madly my father seeks his loves,
with whom there is no standing,
for as he would own himself
he is the measuring rod,
and slowly owes himself to God,
giving of himself with forced breath.

In Limbo

I have a child in limbo
I must bring back.
My experience grows
but there is no wisdom
without a child in the house.

Sunday at the State Hospital

I am sitting across the table
eating my visit sandwich.
The one I brought him stays suspended
near his mouth; his eyes focus
on the table and seem to think,
his shoulders hunched forward.
I chew methodically,
pretending to take him
as a matter of course.
The sandwich tastes mad
and I keep chewing.
My past is sitting in front of me
filled with itself
and trying with almost no success
to bring the present to its mouth.

Mother and Child

She feared the baby would fall.
Upside down she held it.
She loved her child.
As a born baby, it was a practical thing,
handled by doctors. As a drowned baby,
it still would exist.

By accident it died inside its tub.
She carried it carefully to its crib
and there rocked it, as she called for help.
Help, help, she called.
Help, help, she whispered,
hands resting upon her.

Walt Whitman in the Civil War Hospitals

Prescient, my hands soothing
their foreheads, by my love
I earn them. In their presence
I am wretched as death. They smile
to me of love. They cheer me
and I smile. These are stones
in the catapulting world;
they fly, bury themselves in flesh,
in a wall, in earth; in midair
break against each other
and are without sound.
I sent them catapulting.
They outflew my voice
towards vacant spaces,
but I have called them farther,
to the stillness beyond,
to death which I have praised.

SECTION TWO

My Only Enemy

My only enemy has no metal for his hatred,
it comes invisible;

and if I were not indisposed
you would not know I am attacked.
I will die but not at his doing.
It will take my aging friends,
the moon and stars; they are my laughter.
In their light I am disarmed,
sterile to their intelligence.
That is me,
that is how I'll die.
I do not forget my only enemy.

The Orange Picker

I was tempted to the grove by its odor;
the tang lingered over the whole countryside,
and from the hilltop where I stood orange
was the banner laid out like a signal.
I had no exact notion, but of itself
it seemed a goal: to be overwhelmed
in its odor.
                    I came downhill,
and saw these men at work,
on ladders to pick oranges;
they were not tall enough;
and as I watched I too was drawn in.
And now as I labor, the days going by redolent—
I have breathed in them too long to be curious—
these oranges have failed me.

c. 1940

Self-Centered

I love the only day that I was born,
as if in my oneness I could love another,
and yet I love a day. As of the beginning

I am here, but have come really
from the second day in which a sky was made.
Before everything I was what I do not know,
an absence, a beginning. There has been none
since the start. Therefore to love my only day
is to be set apart,
and this what I do when I am one,
and there is what has been,
at which time I was the beginning.

Guilt

Guilt is my one attachment to reality,
for having failed at so much
that now when I refer myself to those failures
I consider life to be formed on these terms;
so that when I am joyful at all I know
for sure that somewhere I have strayed.
My joys are infinite and give my faults
their power to rule me at the end so strongly,
I fly so high and far, that when I am returned
it is to feel that as far as I have flown
that too is the extent of my fault.

c. 1942

Be Like Me

I will walk, if I must,
in a crowd, so that I am kind.
I cannot think, as if I had lost
something that love comes from.
I do not even know
to whom I am talking.
I break off and try to revise.

Someone comes by and whispers,
"Be like me."

A Man

A man confronted by masks
begins to maneuver
out of their reach.
With satisfaction
he sees one fall
as if it had been struck;
it lies crumpled.
He hears weeping,
someone loved
is now a cause for tears.

The Prodigal Son

I went back for redress,
I would show my father
how much better I could act
in his place, and when I had bound
myself to his circumstance
I found my only satisfaction
in setting him
adrift.

The Escapade

Poet and gangster reach in the dark;
blind flashes reveal them.
The dead collapse and the living scatter
for cover. Alone now, they think the street

is theirs and swiftly they make their getaway,
in the left hand the haul, in the right
jammed in the driver's back the weapon
as they career; and at the hideout set up
to repel the law—coming nearly as swift
sirening. In the inferno, started by both sides,
riddled, still seeking to shoot,
they sink to their deaths,
the haul beside them still theirs.

And Step

I understand myself
in relation to a stone,
flesh and bone.
Shall I bow down
to stone? Mine
is the voice
I hear. I will
stand up to stone.
I will be proud
and fragile, I will
be personable
and step over
stone.

I Stand Upon a Dike

I stand upon a dike at night, watching
over the sea's extreme edge sparse settled lights
snap like traffic signals. The ocean
is a darkened ballroom lacking the Saturday night
        crowd;
the place is sad.

from Say Pardon *(1961)* 135

Below me a wave out of the darkness
rushes through a pile of rocks
and sucks them down. Where is the ocean,
the strength of the wave? I see only foam,
white raving, white eyes of nothing.

The wave recedes into the dark for its impetus;
it lashes out from a silent poise,
it sucks down the rocks, hurls spray at me.
It makes me crouch; I cannot shame it,
it has no eyes nor ears.
I cannot die victorious from its beating,
it has no argument.
It races out of the dark knowing nothing,
and I have only this dike.

c. 1938

Content

I should be content
to look at a mountain
for what it is
and not as a comment
on my life.

The Good Angel

Time and again he would come
to give his impossible conditions.
I'd shrug. He'd plead, command,
Do as I say and I will lead your life;
you will float on that shining cloud.
I will do it because I love you,
you are pitiful. And I'd look at him.
Those conditions he would impose on me—

I'd tell him bitterly about them.
He'd try to explain. He was to be won
under those terms, as he understood himself.
I'd continue on my hopeless way,
from home to work and back.
I would see men carefree and fresh
and I'd know they had done the impossible.
At home I found him under my dining table,
asleep and snoring in careless disregard.
I was angry. How could he taunt me,
dying for his favors? I kicked him
and he sprang up and flung his arms apart
and said, At last!

Blessing Myself

I believe in stillness,
I close a door
and surrender myself
to a wall and converse
with it and ask it
to bless me.
The wall is silent.
I speak for it,
blessing myself.

Awaiting

A man with head lifted stands listening
for a sound in an empty field.
He thinks he hears a voice
and is straining to make out
what it is saying.
It is no hallucination
and he stands awaiting
clarification.

All Comes

All comes to sunlight.
A bird stirring its wings.
In the air it has the shape of a dream.
It too is perfect off the ground,
I follow its flight.

Whistle or Hoot

The bird that sings to itself
is never a lonely or frightened bird;
though if before it were silent,
darting its head for worms
or worrisome matters,
now that it sings to itself
it triumphs, whistle or hoot.

Like a Lie

In myself I speak the language of love
and to the outside, of practical matters
because I do not wish to make the truth
sound like a lie.

No Answer

I have learned to love without explanation
for even as I kneel
under a dreadful claw
I yet have the ease
without which I can expect
no answer.

Everybody Knows

The flowers we forget to buy
on birthdays, so busy with everything—
we retrace our steps to say something
apologetic.
            And the flowers we do buy;
everybody knows what flowers cost.

Brief Elegy

In every beautiful song is a promise of sleep.
I will sleep if you will sing to me,
but sing to me of sleep
when the bells have hushed in the towers
and the towers have hushed from their sounds.
Sing to me, strolling through silent streets.

This Is Mortal

The lit room is blinding.
We are moments of the heart.
There is a silence between beats,
no beat for the same blood twice.
We love one another like the motion
of the blood, and there is no outcry,
for this is mortal
in the bright room.

With the Door Open

Something I want to communicate to you,
I keep my door open between us.
I am unable to say it,

I am happy only
with the door open between us.

The Lover

I'd tell of stones dropping upon me
from a high mountain, but to leave
is to lose a mountain and to stay
is to cry, Let me go away.
I would know if you were to stop
suddenly from hurling your stones
and remained perfectly still and cold
in my presence. Then I would leave
humiliated, seeking for something
to be aware of me, even in anger,
as you are. But such anger—
why am I made aware of it
and why does it prolong its torture of me
if its purpose is to be rid of me?
That question keeps me rooted
beneath your height on which I see the sun
dazzle my eyes, as though everything
were well and behovely.

Apple Watcher

Rose is my apple watcher
sitting in a tree
and I watch Rose
counting apples
she believes in.
She smiles the whole crop in
and the one she throws me
as the best I believe
even if it will not chew

because I too am smiled in,
just like you,
old battered skin.

SECTION THREE

The Mountain Is Stripped

I no longer have to declare myself;
a quietness urges me, regardless
of my grievance, to go about.
I affect the justice of my cause;
while I live I am the answer to harm.

I have been made frail with righteousness:
with two voices. I am but one person.
The warning voice is God:
the whales are bled in the sea,
the mountain is stripped.

I Felt

I felt I had met the Lord.
He calmed me, calling me
to look into my child's room.
He said, I am love,
and you will win your life
out of my hands
by taking up your child.

from Say Pardon *(1961)* 141

Without Fear

I weep to myself
and I ask if this self-pity,
terror and love are not enough
to preserve us, and I think
then that all will be well.
Without fear of contradiction,
I give you God in my life.

And I Stand

Behind my enemy stands God,
watching how near I come
to killing, to making
my own world and time,
and then ask His love.
And I stand and gaze
past my enemy at Him.

I Shall Follow

I shall follow
as the shadow that has mountains
in its path. You are undeformed
by these imperceptions, and I shall not be
constrained either in pursuit,
attached to you as an emanation is.
This is how I shall complete my happiness,
in you.

For the Living

Said the Lord, I am humble
of my powers and you
who are proud I will let live
as long as my humility abides
which is forever—
but I have proclaimed judgment
against you.

Noah

He must wade out to a high point
and build an ark of the trees,
take two of each kind of happiness.
And send out
a pigeon that shall not return,
after the bubbling shriek of the drowned;
it shall land upon a rock.
God of his crying shall have made the flood subside.
He shall emerge
upon the earth, brown for grief
of its dead, and know no better
than before, save there is a promise
to cling to when the floods rise.

God Said

God said, Have you finished my thinking?
Now think yourself into stone
and I will lift you
and set you upon a mountain.

Samson

Did I love God for myself alone
or for my enemies' sake also
that I might not despair of God's goodness?
With the jawbone of an ass
I had killed contemptuously.
I loved Delilah and I would teach her
His love that she might go and speak
to them in earnest and she did speak
and I pulled the pillars down
one by one in bitter surprise
that goodness could give my enemy
triumph.

A Semblance

Over your mother's grave
speak a prayer of bafflement,
grasp the hand of the rabbi,
nearest to steady you.
He recites the prayer
for you to follow unsteadily
its meaning. You pray
to the air.

Job's Anger

It was not a man's way to plead
with God. Strength and will
had built his house. He would
bring God down and he cursed
and challenged God
to make Himself known
and to defend Himself

from Job's anger
that strength and will
were not enough,
and God came down.

The Rightful One

I heard my son burst out of his room
and shout, he is here, dad. He is here.
I understood and I managed to stand up,
melting within, and walk the hall
between our rooms to meet Him
whom I had neglected in my thoughts;
but not my son who was ill
and had searched for Him.
He had come. I saw Him standing,
his hair long, face exhausted, eyes sad
and knowing, and I bent my knee,
terrified at the reality,
but he restrained me with a hand
and said, I am a sufferer like yourself.
I have come to let you know.
And I arose, my heart swelling, and said,
I have failed and bitterness is in me.
And he replied, And forgiveness too.
Bless your son. And I blessed him
and his face brightened. And the Rightful One
was gone and left a power to feel free.

PART SEVEN

Poems of the 1960's

The Journey

I am looking for a past
I can rely on
in order to look to death
with equanimity.
What was given me:
my mother's largeness
to protect me,
my father's regularity
in coming home from work
at night, his opening the door
silently and smiling,
pleased to be back
and the lights on
in all the rooms
through which I could run
freely or sit at ease
at table and do my homework
undisturbed: love arranged
as order directed at the next day.
Going to bed was a journey.

A Loose Gown

I wear my life loosely around me,
feeling it at elbows and knees.
Sometimes I'm forced to hurry
and it races along with me,
taking the wind in its hollows.
I get out of breath
and would fall down exhausted
but the wind in these pockets
of my life keep me from falling.

A Glimpse of e. e. cummings

The reading was over and he stood against
The rear wall, head up, keeping a smile,
being talked to. One more chore
for the money and he could have been
enjoying it for the challenge to the self
his smile protected. A girl student
spoke to his face. He nodded
and in a moment answered quietly
and quickly in a high-pitched voice.
Was it this vocal weakness he meant
to shield as the self, because it was
so awkward in him? He meant nothing
more after that but to listen,
to nod and smile at each body
in turn taking a stand before him.
I hung about watching and studying
his face for the poems being written
there at that moment and found it
weary but alert,
aged
and loving defiance.

Poems the Dead Know by Heart

Long poems are for the dead
whose eyes are closed
to the shortness of life;
they know everything by heart,
and the poem sings itself
in their naked bones.
They are the long poem concluded,
that began with the skull
and reached to the toes.
The body lived until no longer
needed, the poem then put
between covers.

Directive

Break the branch,
break it.
What is there to fear?
Break, break,
you are living,
aren't you?
Alive and you have fears.
They consist of this breaking
for you are of this happening
too, whether or not
it happens with you.
Break and be the one
who has it in his hand.

If flowers want to grow
right out of the concrete sidewalk cracks
I'm going to bend down to smell them.

In an Open Palm

I see myself at my own feet,
dead of my own error in judgment.
I was gentle and I was negligent
believing in life:
defeat was to find me living
calmly in my house, writing
steadily.
   Oh death did not
neglect to find me, entered
through the eye and ear
as I waited for morning
and it was humans wronging
one another and growing hard

and strong and taking my bowels
and bones unto themselves,
and now I stand guarding
a fallen friend, in death.
I will defend his right
to the funeral speech
on his virtue. I alone
will place him in the grave
and set a stone above him,
carved as a lion
crouching in an open palm.

In Childhood

In the lumberyard where I stood
I held up a small round hand mirror
to the sun and let its rays strike
at an angle directed at a shadowed wall
which now lit up the size of a mirror.
I then bent to collect stamps
off old discarded envelopes scattered
across the yard. Someday I would
travel to those scenes on the stamps
and talk to people there. We would
celebrate my coming from miles away
for I now knew light could reach
across dark distance.

The Integers

Let me hold your body
while computers spin
in their circuits,
devising a fabric

of mathematics
out of our skin.

My tongue twists around "two"
and will not uncurl
to say, You and me.

My fingers are ten,
making ten places
on your skin.
My lips are two,
imprinting on yours
my one excited heart.

I am the shape of "one"
and as I bend my knees
to you lying upon a bed
and make the shape of "two"
your legs encircle my body
in the sign of infinity.

Leaping from Ambush

A man goes by with a woman.
Another man cleaning his car
by the curb glances at her
and follows with his eyes
but returns to wiping his car
with a chamois cloth.
                              Is it
the chamois cloth that stops him
from killing the man and leaping
upon the woman?

Falling Asleep Thinking of Teeth

Do I need teeth, I ask myself in sleep,
perfectly calm. I am loved by my daughter,
not for the sake of my teeth, but if these
are mine what have I got against them,
another side of me wants to know,
in my sleep. I am being taken over
by two calm but contending thoughts.

I dream controversially.
Being old and unattractive
but faithfully loved would solve problems.
I would look around freely
and make notes, come upon secrets
that would make people shout
in surprise.
                    Now what could such secrets
be, I ask myself in my sleep, calmly.
No answer. I am asleep.

The Night Life

This time from behind
in enmity
to destroy love
in an ecstasy
without love
I grasp you
with brutal force
of the gained self
Love I shout with derision
with each thrust
Love love love
my voice reaches
higher and higher
till love is thrust open

at the top
and lets me in
like a mad monk
humble and shaking.

Steps for Three—A Prose Poem

On stage, a girl child, father and mother sit around a
table silently looking at each other. The child stretches
out an arm to the father who in turn reaches towards his
wife. She lifts both arms in opposite directions completing
the circle. There is a slight swaying from side to side as
they sit at ease. A radio plays jazz. They stand up and
walk around the table stately and slow as in a dance,
expressing a restrained joy. Suddenly the child breaks
away to dance an ecstatic pleasure in herself. The parents
continue their stately movements but have fixed each
other in a stare. The child breaks off her whirling to rush
back and join them but is prevented by the grip they
have taken on each other's wrists. She rushes away to
struggle with her emotions, her arms weave torturedly
around her body and head. She runs headlong back to
fling herself upon their hands. Their grip broken, they
come forward each in an orbit of the self. The child runs
from one to the other, in a vain effort to reach a hand,
then backs away to begin an orbit of her own, speeding
it up as in a frenzy.

One by one the three figures collapse in exhaustion, with
outstretched arms and inadvertently touching hands leap
away. They are making painful exits off the stage on
their stomachs, crawling in different directions. The stage
empties, the radio jazz stops and the announcer's voice
rises in excitement and dies away. In the silence and
emptiness, the girl child returns slowly, dancing the mo-
tions of longing and nostalgia. The mother follows lan-
guidly, arms wrapped around her eyes to fling them wide

in a tragic and irremediable gesture, as she dances. She does not see the child. The father makes his way back on stage in short, rigid steps, erratically. He keeps himself erect under severe tension. When finally he reaches stage front, he stands perfectly still, staring out at the audience. The mother and child without realizing weave around him in their depression, self-absorbed, but as they pass each other, accidentally touching hands, they pause to look, part, then as they complete another circle touch again, pause, part to meet again and hold hands and to dance together tentatively. Their movements as they grow more sure of each other become light and joyous and take on the gestures of a celebration, while he remains rigid and still. At the height of their excitement and pleasure, almost an ecstasy—they sway from the hips, their arms raised above their heads in abandon—he makes small, abrupt mechanical turns of his body.

The Last Attempt

I have still to sort you out from my dream;
a face looms on mine,
as it were an answer
around which I would bend my will.
Stagger me with your contempt,
I reject death to live the faults
of this world for their failures
as constituting death. Unhappy,
you see yourself only to be loved
by an unhappy man. I tell you,
contemptuous of us both,
we are the life and the way.

The Stake and the Chain

I heard you tell me candid expressions of defeat
within your own home as we zipped by the marshes
of New Jersey. Bus tires roared through your talk.
You were pretty to look at in profile
at the window, the fields swimming backwards.
I wondered what kind of life you and I
would have lived together. We had
bafflements in common and I could see
myself in love with you, and already
I loved what you said and the way
it was being said, with that simplicity
of self that asked a sharing in defense
of life.
      I said little, except to nod
and say I understood, repeated myself,
enchanted, afraid of love. It was love
we were discussing in sad retrospect,
and love before us yet to be,
my breath short, caught up,
my heart hastening me.

But we were past being impulsive,
with the stake driven deep into the past
and the chain grown shorter
with the passing days, love aging
between us and life forever young,
the roaring bus bouncing,
the stop approaching
to get off.

1960

My son, my only death,
I give you your money
for the week. I leave,

happy and unhappy,
lightheaded, bewildered
at myself. Am I betrayed?
Where am I going without him?

I am alone here among trees and fields.
We were together and I loved your pauses
and difficulty in speaking.
I was warmed by your problem,
a man who would speak calmly,
making decision. I was all for that.

You came from behind doors
unlocked for you, remained silent
until I grew silent
and then you spoke
of the one in you
hidden away
to whom you owe much
and who will come for that reason
and demand you entirely.

It is peace coming to claim you,
your face laboring and grave.

Love Poem for the Forty-Second Street Library

With my eyes turned to the sky
and my toes nearly touching pavement,
floating along I'll approach Times Square,
the cabs coming to a screeching halt,
whistles blowing and crowds on four corners
huddled together and staring,
my legs trailing above the ground,
my eyes lifted entranced
to the top of the Empire State Building
as they stare unbelievingly,

attaché cases and handbags weighing
them down, their backs aching.
I'll turn my shimmering gaze towards the Library,
my love for it spreading to the crowds
which will begin to sway softly and sing
to themselves of better days that have passed
and been forgotten. Children once with eyes
for everything, now their eyes on the dollar
which too hovers in front of them.

I'll glide up Fifth Avenue, my eyes focused
longingly on Central Park, on perhaps one small corner
where I will lie down and meditate,
and no crowds but each of us
spread in his favorite spot of lawn
or nearby shrub. I'll be followed
like the Holy Grail and later
go to jail for stopping traffic.
I'll turn my eyes upwards to the ceiling.
The warden and his wards will look
upwards with me in curiosity.

Oh judge, I'll plead, my toes trailing
the courtroom floor, I've been happy
this way, my eyes shimmering and turned
upwards to all things.

For the Night

Look ma, I'm not your son any longer,
with sore lips and hungry belly
whining for satisfaction. I'm not
someone you can put down as a pest
like so many, including your husband
and yourself, with backaches
climbing up and down the basement
stairway to mind the furnace.

I changed myself into an angel
by sitting and thinking
and now you can go tell your neighbors
and all our relatives I've made something
of myself at last.
                    True, true, my light
closes down for the night, for it's work
again for me next morning. I've got
a job at last bringing home the buck
for rent. But I am a beacon of light
after supper, when I stretch out on the couch
and think myself into a trance,
as I look inside for the real me.

I wish it were a joke I was talking about.
Outside the only thing I feel or hear or see
is the bus traveling its route uptown,
then turning into the car barn
for the night.

Where Nothing Is Hidden

Now I understand myself running back
to the city, out of breath and happy
to have escaped the sight of green vomit
and the groaning power lawn mower—
this advertised peace. I wanted
truly undisguised faces of boredom
swirling around me in the street
and my own grim hail to traffic jams,
to death by cops' cross fire,
to dope addiction,
to married life in Brooklyn overlooking the cemeteries
and to the crumbling beer-can-littered schoolyards
of Harlem.
Nothing is hidden.
Nobody lies or covers up.

A low gas cloud covers the city
on which the people slowly choke in bed
but not one's own green vomit to walk on
in silence. It hangs a curtain from the trees.

Scream and yell and pound on the walls here in
        the city,
to be ignored or beaten down.
Speak of the bitter with your last breath
and sweep the whole city into the sea
with a gesture or drive your car off the dock,
taking with you the city's death,
but none of the green vomit
of those who spill their guts
and stand on it in silence like trees
that hide their birds from one another
and live for hundreds of years
without comment.

Country Living

Here it's so quiet I can't hear
a car crash or a gun fire
or an addict groan, so perhaps
I'll give myself a good time
by slashing my wrist
or screaming out the window
for help from trees or squirrels.
I expect a neighbor's dog
running freely through the yards
in search of bones or playmates
will race up to my window and bark
at me competing with him;
and if I should be led away
to be examined I'd offer to return
to the city where I'd be normal indeed
crossing against traffic

or looking for a female
in a drunken bar.

The Blue Danube

What about your death?
Is that my problem too?
They're sending rockets to the moon, I mean,
but no one yet has sent a messenger to me,
telling me I'm me. I mean, how long is this
going to go on? When will crowds wave hello
and I begin smiling and laughing and talking
back? I mean, I do have a life I can call
mine?
            I bought groceries today and found
myself at the head of a line stretching
to the rear of the store but that was
after waiting thirty minutes to move up.
I mean I take this stuff home and eat it,
and you were on the line with me
when you threw up your hands
and started to shout Help,
and the amplifier system was playing softly
The Blue Danube
and I was about to fall asleep
on my feet.

Emergency Clinic II

Your eyes were bulging behind thick horn-rimmed
            glasses
and you smelled of liquor, staring at me speechlessly
above wet, protruberant lips. You kept up your head
with difficulty, slowly slipping down the chair.
I heard you mutter God, once, and turn your head

to stare silently and dazedly at the side wall.
I kept addressing you, seeking answers
to my questions about your child, ill
of pneumonia in the waiting room, its mother
at its side. Why drunk at such a time?
But I assumed you drank regularly and heavily.
I typed the answers as you gave them,
after repeated questioning and waiting.
Your eyes dropped and closed, then struggled open
on a blank face.
                    You had some learning,
from the neat clipped speech and complete sentences
you did manage to speak. You got to your feet,
after bracing yourself on the arms of the chair,
then sighing with the effort to stand left
without another word or glance, still struggling
to keep your head from falling between your shoulders.
I forgot about you, relieved as you left,
taking the fumes with you. I admitted another
patient and slipped into the lobby with my records
to take an elevator to the wards. Your wife
was there waiting too, with the child in her arms,
as you stood swaying beside her,
and she swayed, hers the bleary face
of a heavy drinker too
who looked at me blankly
as if waiting for a comment on your lives.

Off to the Cemetery

> To die is to be brought down among blacks
> and Puerto Ricans who live in rat buildings
> and inject themselves to endure
> the wastes of newsprint in the street.
> To die is to be abandoned to the Sanitation
> Department that comes to remove you

quickly in an oblong garbage box,
the men ashamed of their uniforms.

The funeral is attended with studied
preparations for a wedding. The event
grows happy and relieved as it concludes
and the body is removed from the chapel.
Then all get to file out. The ceremony
was not to see the departed off
to an eternal rest, life transitory
if blessed, but for a pact, a vow
of renewed heat, life married to death
and made one, and away the guests go
to the cemetery in cars and cabs
that are as good-looking as false teeth.

Headline: Prisoner Without Remorse

> Why did you kill? Did you have a quarrel?
>
> I had no quarrel.
>
> Did he have the stuff you needed for a fix?
>
> I had plenty of stuff.
>
> Then why did you kill him?
>
> To make him cry.
>
> Why did you want to make him cry?
>
> I wanted to see how it felt for someone else to
> cry.
>
> And did you find out?
>
> Yes, I found out.
>
> It was bad.
>
> It was very bad.

And now he is dead, and that is the result
of your curiosity.

We both die and I am glad.

Then you know you must die for this.

Yes, I know.

Do you have no remorse or regret for killing
your friend?

I have no regret or remorse. We were friends.
What was to happen to him was to happen to
        me too.
We were very close.

And now he is dead.

Yes, and now I die like him and he is not angry
and I am not angry. It is just right to die.

The Appointment Card

He flashes a knife and waves it under our noses
as he sways from seat to seat where passengers sit
quietly waiting for him to pass by. He curses us
and leers and makes menacing gestures of cutting up
into small pieces each and every one of us.
We watch, we wait. Soon, soon the train will reach
its stop and we'll get off. He strikes a face.
The person screams and collapses. The knifer
stands over him, looking down, waiting to decide,
waiting for his thought. Perhaps it is the person
on the floor who must act it out for him.
If he gets up, stab again. If he moans, stab again.
If he seeks to crawl away whimpering and begging
not to be touched again, strike anyhow.
The rest of us seated look on,
frozen by a sudden recognition of absurdity.

Is this the brutality and horror
which we feared until now and is not feared any longer,
so ordinary compared to what we feared? Let it pass.
Let this worst pass. It could be worse still.
Let us continue to live humiliated
and defeated because there is nothing to rebel against,
the cause mundane, a life, another life, another death
and defeat.
        I am anxious to get off the train to think
about myself. The train stops, the doors open
and the knifer is caught as he begins to leave.
He is beaten and dragged out and the stabbed person
bleeding on the floor is placed on a stretcher
and carried away. The train moves past me
and out of the station.
        I wish I knew where I
was going gladly, as it says on my appointment card.
I wish I could say I was going there as I go
trembling. The train has left me behind
to find my way upstairs to an exit,
the card a piece of paper in my hand.

The businessman is a traitor to himself first
of all and then no one else matters,
hardened, sick of himself.
        I once knew
someone like that and he died in a chair.
It was sad for the chair, sold
and nobody knows now who has it.
The funeral had ten Cadillacs
filled with friends. I was there.
I was last to talk to him
or rather he talked to me
and said, I've got a big deal on
and want you in on it.

Cash and Carry

Dear pop, you might like to know: your death
has brought back good times. I now have money
for taxes and a couple of dollars left
each month to put on my account.

I can see your half-sardonic smile,
thinking, Yep, it's me again helping him.
You're right, pop, and I did work hard
to support you too in your last days,
ten thousand dollars' worth of debts,
your sick bills, and now you're gone,
leaving me to clean up and to get back
into shape, I hope. Oh yes, arguing
back and forth who was right,
we had some fun together.

Prayer

May I continue to earn money
to pay my bills
so that I have the peace
to write at leisure of arrangements
between us that have life for a name
and are taken seriously by bill collectors
earning commission.

Reversals

I have trained myself in idleness and want.
My days are spent in reaching for shadows.
I have an eye for the sun, the moon,
the clouds, for trees in bloom,
for sidewalks broken up by rain and snow,

for old red frame houses
with small nineteenth-century windows
on abandoned corners among warehouses
and garages, beside oily waterfronts
and the once modish homes of retired sailors
who spent their last days overlooking the ships
incoming and outgoing, white sails full.
I have an eye for abandoned lots let to rubbish
and weeds among slanted shanty homes.
In these lots are torn tires, tops to garbage cans
and broken beer cartons. I look over everything
lovingly and the children who play among them
in their torn stockings and soiled dresses
and pants, quiet children with blond hair
and blue eyes speaking in the accents
of their parents' native tongue,
and when I come to the new office buildings
and the factories set up in midst of these forgotten
things I am repelled and challenged
in my inmost slothful lazy self. Naturally
I respond by straightening up and brightening
my face before I am seen and adjusting
my language and my thoughts for the moment
I step into these new structures but I know
what I'll say at a given moment and how
the others will respond. I know exactly
how the day will end there, with tired conviviality
and spread goodnights, each of us energetic
beyond our normal means, as we push out
into the street towards home. On the way
back through the forgotten neighborhood
I look again for the stout plain mothers
on the wooden steps of their frame houses
looking out for their children in weed lots.
I am calmed, returned to my simplicity
and unpretentious self. I am made fearful
and depressed, shown death and neglect.
I am shown my secret thoughts, my true motivation.
I am shown my flight into money.

Hunger on TV

I

We touch eyes
through a screen
where your gaunt lips
wish to smile
at my offered hand.
I feed my self-pity.

I am a governmental policy
perpetuating you
in the woman beneath me
who will make another
child to replace you
damaged beyond repair.

I too am leaving the earth,
rising into the dark
of my disbelief.
I want your real hand
as we float free
in the dark spaces
of a negative world.

II

The Child Responds

Alone, I have no reason to believe
others live for me.
                    I float along
keeping myself upright
in space everywhere empty.
Drawn to the sun
I will turn satellite
burned out
and idly orbiting
touching others
how they touch me.

The Cookout

A lit charcoal stove stands against the rear wall of the lawn. Children are gathered around to watch the chef putter with spices and dab them on the meat as he turns the spit. Flames crackle and flare and the children shout, rubbing their bellies. In the center of the lawn the adults are grouped around a garden table sipping their drinks in chairs. They talk and yawn, stretch casually and occasionally turn to encourage the chef or jokingly demand he hurry up. He shouts back, "Try it yourself!" as they subside in chuckles. His wife admonishes him airily to be polite and he fires back, "You mean to those hungry wolves!"

There is this contrived congeniality in the air, the conversation is unenlightening but the sounds and gestures express astonishment or concern or thoughtful looks, with deep nodding. Smoke from the charcoal burner drifts across to them and the adults stand up, make signs of pleasure and of hunger, grimace with stomach pains. The children are jumping up and down or holding hands and whirling each other in circles, as they chant, "We're going to eat steak, we're going to eat steak!" The adults clap in rhythm, shouting encouragement. Suddenly the children rush to their parents' sides to tug and haul at them to join the circle and the babble of voices, old and young, grows excited and merry. Reluctantly the parents allow themselves to be drawn in, with laughter, as they form a large ring with the children, but they begin to exhibit their own excitement as they move in measure to the chant. Those adults who had flatly refused to join hands before with the children now join hands among themselves under the influence of their excited peers. They begin a circle of their own in a slow, awkward step to a kind of dance. One woman among them impetuously pulls on the others to speed it up and with shouts urges them on gaily. Their quick, graceful tempo now takes on the air of a celebration. The men, several who have been drinking, weave and twist in the excited woman's steps. They grab at other women who dodge playfully. The circle falls apart as the men persist, the women laughing. They pair off in a game of pursuit. One trips and falls, bringing down her partner on top. He refuses to get up, there is a kind of feverishness now among the adults that is out of control. The larger circle of parents and children by now has also broken up, the children jumping on one another and bringing each other to the ground, bumping the adults who pile up on the grass in laughter and shouts.

The chef has abandoned his stove to look for his wife somewhere in the struggling mass. He keeps shouting her name, demanding to know where she is. He trips over a thrashing leg, falls and is gathered willy-nilly into the swarm. The screams of women mingle with their hysterical giggles as the men's voices rise and fall stertoriously like a roaring herd.

It gradually subsides, as bodies roll apart, exhausted, arms and legs flung wide apart. They smell the odor of burnt meat and jump to their feet, screaming, "The meat is burned!" They pummel each other in anger and disappointment, the children too hitting each other. The chef groggily rises to his feet, spreads wide his arms and shouts, "Where is my hat?"

America America

Someone chops down a tree and begins to saw it into lumber strips. Another man measures the ground with footsteps, preparing a place on which to build a house. He counts his steps aloud. Still another man drives up in a truck, stops and descends to the ground, goes to the rear of the truck and hauls off pipes, wires, bathroom fixtures, etcetera. At this point a fire engine roars up to the scene, its siren screeching. The firemen in rubber coats and boots and with hose in hand jump off, rush the nozzle end of the hose to the water pump nearby, screw it on as other fireman frantically uncoil the rest of the hose from the truck. The water is turned on full force. Cops come sirening up in their patrol cars, act to halt traffic in either direction, there is no traffic, as the hose is played on the ground that had just been measured off and on the prone, half-sawed tree, on the supply truck and on the men who had been working. They stand perfectly still receiving the stream of water on their bodies and faces. Scene ends with everyone coming to the front to take a bow.

I climb up on stage and shake everybody's hand in congratulation, after which I turn the hose on myself, as I quote aloud the Bible, Thou shalt do unto others as thou wouldst have others do unto you.

The cops pull their guns from holsters. Everyone else lies down on the ground, preparing to sleep. They yawn, scratch themselves, talk casually to each other with gestures. The cops look in dismay and turn the guns on themselves but several of the firemen get up from the ground, take the guns away from the cops while shaking their heads in disapproval and turn the guns on themselves. The carpenter, the truck driver, the surveyor get up and take the guns away from the firemen and turn the barrels on themselves. At this, the cops and the firemen raise their hands in joy but the would-be suicides on impulse suddenly turn the guns on the audience and begin firing. The audience fires back. The firemen sing The Star Spangled Banner, the cops salute repeatedly and a very important individual emerges from the backstage to begin a pantomime of an impassioned speech with all the rhetorical flourishes of a trained politician. I have been standing aside all this while, observing the development. Now I ask aloud everybody in the audience to please contribute his or her dime for the Prevention of

Infantile Paralysis, at which I take a bow in self-congratulation and receive a swift inadvertent kick from behind by a fireman who has been dancing.

Learning to Scratch

A stage hand comes out of the wings and yanks the pullcord of a motor. It starts up with a roar but settles immediately into a loud purring rhythm. In the group standing about idly on stage someone begins to shake to the motor's rhythm. A second person gets down on all fours and begins barking at that person and circling around him as if getting ready to attack. A third person goes after the dog one with a stick to drive him off. Now a girl is attracted to the rhythmic movement of the first person and joins him. They synchronize their motions and move around each other as in a dance. Another woman dressed as a nurse comes on stage proudly carrying a newborn baby in her arms and presents it to the girl who takes it in her arms as she keeps up with her "husband." The dog person has freed himself of the one who had been trying to drive him off and now is concentrating his barks and threats on the new mother as he circles around her.

In the meanwhile, congratulations are in order over the newborn child. The other members of the group gather around the dancing couple, raise glasses in salute and begin to sing "Rock-a-by Baby in the Tree Top" as they embrace each of the "married" pair fondly and then leap into each other's arms to play the role of children being cradled and rocked to sleep by parents. The singing grows louder. The sound of the running motor increases in tempo to the increasing volume of singing. The persons who have been playing the role of children in their parents' arms jump down and go through the motions of a tantrum, with appropriate bawling and howls. They approach the motor menacingly, meaning to kick it, when a stroke of stage lightning followed by a clap of thunder stuns them where they stand. They begin to shrink back. The same stagehand who had yanked the pullcord returns on stage and pulls the ignition cord, stopping the motor which he then wheels offstage.

The couple that has been keeping its rhythm with their feet continue but look around, bewildered by the silence, the woman holding the baby in her arms. The dog person has slouched away into a corner to lick himself, wholly involved with himself now. All the others with drinks in their hands and those who were the "tantrum" children look and feel vacant in their roles, walk around the stage aimlessly, bumping into each other. The stage becomes a vast confusion of milling persons. In the middle the couple with the baby are being bumped and shoved and nearly thrown down as they try bravely to continue to move to the rhythm of the absent motor. The dog actor now has taken to chasing his tail and yipping in glee. He attracts the attention of the aimless, milling crowd and they gather to watch him. One drops to the stage floor on all fours and imitates the dog person. The girl who had been standing beside him hastens to follow and they circle around each other, chasing their imaginary tails and yipping and barking with delight and nuzzling each other.

A proud nurse wearing a dog mask comes trotting out on stage with a brand-new puppy in her arms and presents it to the couple on all fours. They take it with yips of joy, as everyone else falls to the floor on all fours also and begins chasing his or her tail—with the exception of the rhythmic couple who don't seem to be able to stop themselves. I, who have been in the audience all this while, very curious, come on stage and look around me and scratch my head in puzzlement, soon finding myself itching as if bitten by fleas and scratching everywhere and making little wordless sounds of pleasure. I finally discover one place that itches most of all to which I give all my

loving attention as I emit a long-drawn-out howl of satis-
faction and release.

Where There Is Life

It was a machine gun firing automatically at the distance,
I approached at an angle on my belly as people fell
where they strolled in the fields. Others looked about for
a cause, puzzled, and knelt to examine the bodies. I
reached the gun finally from the rear and released the
trigger and banged the barrel. There was no cartridge
belt in sight, no ammuniation boxes. It was as if the gun
positioned among the grass were being fed from below.

The shells kept pouring out, the barrel beginning to swerve
from side to side, its shells hitting trees, houses, cars, birds.
I heard screams from all over. Houses bursting into flames
and exploding, their gas tanks hit. The trees ripped through
the middle began to topple. The barrel swerved com-
pletely around and I ducked so fast I struck my head
against the ground.

Dazed, I see planes reconnoiter. The pilot waves me
away. I back off weakly on my belly towards the woods
and soon I see pillars of dirt soar into the air where the
gun stood. The bombing goes on. It is more than I can
take. Trees shake so hard their leaves fall and bury me
beneath them where I lie, pressed against the earth face
down. In the silence as the bombing finally stops, I begin
to make out the gun still rattling away, but now there is
a rat-tat from everywhere, even in the woods, as if guns
had sprung up like mushrooms after rain. I keep lying
here very still, not daring to move, my joints in their
fixed awkward position, as if having grown old.

A First on TV

(For Walter Cronkite)

This is the twentieth century,
you are there, preparing to skin
a human being alive. Your part
will be to remain calm
and to participate with the flayer
in his work as you follow his hand,
the slow, delicate way with the knife
between the skin and flesh,
and see the red meat emerge.
Tiny rivulets of blood will flow
from the naked flesh and over the hands
of the flayer. Your eyes will waver
and turn away but turn back to witness
the unprecedented, the incredible,
for you are there
and your part will be to remain calm.

You will smash at the screen
with your fist and try to reach
this program on the phone, like a madman
gripping it by the neck
as it were the neck of the flayer
and you will scream into the receiver,
"Get me Station ZXY at once, at once,
do you hear!" But your part
will be to remain calm.

A Political Cartoon

Ten men are seated around a conference table, each with
a sign attached to the back of the head giving his title.
However, each stands up in turn to identify himself. "I
am the Secretary of the Interior." "I am the Secretary of
the Treasury." "I am the Secretary of Agriculture." "I

am the Secretary of Housing and Urban Development."
"Secretary of Commerce." "Health, Education and Wel-
fare." And so on. Finally, a slow, deliberative figure rises
to his feet and announces solemnly that he is the President.

He sits down with dignity. A gun is lying in front of him
on the table. He shakes his head at it sorrowfully and
pushes it gently across the table to the Secretary of the
Interior, who cocks the gun and pushes it carefully to the
Secretary of Commerce seated beside him. The Secretary
of Commerce fondles it and puts it to his ear as if listening
for a sound of life and then shoves it across the table to
the Attorney General, who takes it and holds it up to his
eyes admiringly, turning it over and over in his hands.
He thrusts it at the Secretary of State, who pulls back
alarmed but then manages to take it in his nervous hands.
He has made the others smile and laugh softly. A joking
undercurrent makes itself felt. He bravely twirls the gun
around his finger, striking a nonchalant pose, one arm
draped across the back of his chair. The gun whirls off
his finger and is caught with both hands with a shout of
fright by the Secretary of Health, Education and Welfare
at whom the gun has been flying. As he catches it with
almost a comical motion laughter explodes around the
table, joined in by the President who however is shaking
his head in disapproval.

Now the gun is being passed rapidly from hand to hand
as in a game of bean bag. It suddenly fires, sending
everyone diving beneath the table except the Secretary of
the Interior. He is slumped across the table, blood
spreading over its surface. Some time passes before the
others come up from beneath the table and reseat them-
selves. They stare at the dead man. The President, sitting
erect and firmly in his chair, has resumed the dignity of
his office. Again the gun lies in front of him and he
plays with it idly, musing, sad and grim. He shakes his
head, holds the gun up to his eyes and examines it with
distaste, then stands up slowly, a hand upon his chest.

He begins silently to mouth his words in a speech addressed to the Cabinet, his free hand pointing tragically at the weapon lying on the table in front of him. Following a long peroration with appropriate gestures, he turns his attention to the gun, talking directly at it in accusatory style, climaxed by an imperious gesture of his thumb for the weapon to leave the room. He then sits down in exhaustion and mops his brow. With anger and disgust he pushes the gun across the table to the Attorney General, who slides it gently towards the Secretary of Agriculture. It goes the round of the table and just as it is about to be returned to the President it goes off again. The Secretary of Commerce falls back against his chair, his head drops loosely onto his shoulder. He is dead. All the others bow their heads and clasp their hands on the table in front of them in sorrowful prayer.

The silence suddenly is shattered by the blare of a truck horn outside behind the conference room door. The double doors roll up like garage doors to show a real truck standing behind them, its motor racing and backfiring. The truck rolls in and circles the room, its chassis heaped with grain. The truck stops and backs up against the table between the President and the Secretary of Agriculture and begins to unload, tipping the chassis upwards. The grain slides down, burying beneath it the table, up to the waist of everyone seated around it. The President, in the meanwhile, has dug the gun out of the grain from in front of the body of the Secretary of Commerce and hands it without comment to the Secretary of Health, Education and Welfare, who accepts it with a grave nod and gives it to the Secretary of State. It starts to make the rounds of the table again. It is also offered to the two dead gentlemen as a token of lasting respect. In the meantime, the truck has left empty while another has backed into the room with still another load. It too is deposited upon the conference table and the cabinet members are buried beneath it over their heads, except for the President who has received the gun and is standing and firing deliberately and with dignity, until he too is buried above his head, including his upraised hand gripping the gun. All the while it is I who have been driving the truck into the conference room and spilling the grain.

My Native Land

I pledge allegiance to the lips of the vagina,
I swear by it and kiss its flag.
I live in that country and would be buried there,
proud of its passivity. In such a place
I could live forever but since I must die
I would let my praise live on
for I am strange to myself,
seeing that I come from between two lips
and a beard, farther in a land
pink, tender, wet and lacking air,
close-clinging,
making me breathless
as I grow in it and die of pleasure.

Hardly like America.

Us

This country—
people in it in their cars,
the silos stuffed with wheat off the roads.
Missiles stand ready
to empty the world of us.

1965

I have the Vietnam blues and greys
fought for ground to pieces
by cannon sightseers visit today
an American barracks blows up
with a hundred men in it was no joke
on us who thought we had it made
quite a stink back home they sat
at their television sets wear out
get out people cry long and hard
over your wounded he managed to get up
and fire his burp gun at the enemy
before dying he took ten men
with him went farmers mechanics husbands
and sons whose mothers work in gun factories.

All the atom bombs and bombers,
the microbes and the gases,
the psychologists and the pamphleteers,
the propagandists, the spies
and the provocateurs, the double agents
and the undercover men
mean well by us and intend
harm only to the harmful
and believe in man
just as you and I do,
born of man and with man's powers
and faults and so I reach out
with love and understanding
to which they will respond
in kind and lose themselves
in their love, as I will
in my love for them.
Amen.

Moonlight Poem

I wish you would get happy again
so I could knock it out of you.
It's a way of entertaining myself
because I can't stand
your beatific face
in the moonlight.

The Secret Crumbs

The execution was pronounced in the womb,
so it is how I feel without surprise
or anger, being led by my blood.

I sleep, resigning myself.
I am older then when I was a child,
I am hard-looking,
I want to die full of truth
which will keep the earth fresh
on top of me.
                    •
            The body is dead
and mice nibble at it and flee
at the sound of approaching feet.

The body is dead and mice take in their mouths
a piece to nourish themselves away from the body
in their secret holes to breed more mice,
but the body that defied them
and kept them in their walls to nibble at plaster
and secret crumbs is dead
and the mice take the body into their mouths
boldly piece by piece and take over the floor
where the skeleton lies
and become a body unto themselves
and turn on themselves in fright
and eat one another angrily.

A Case History

Lately my asshole has been talking to me
about the world. I feel it pouting its lips
and I have to spread my cheeks to get the words
clearly. I have been astonished as anyone
might be and embarrassed to talk about it
to others. I had thought of seeing a doctor
but my anus said, To hell with the doctor,
listen to me. I am here at the center of things
and can tell you plenty that goes on in the dark
unbeknown to you, how things are turned into crap
and then passed out and forgotten, the best of
    them.
The finest fruits and vegetables, the sweetest cakes
the smoothest liquers—
all, all pass through and are destroyed
and made shit of and never seen again
nor heard from, leaving nothing of themselves behind.
Nothing, nothing of any use at all.

I listen to its rumbling and farting between words,
under covers fearfully to let no one else hear
and think me mad, and I have begun holding
    conversations
with it lately, asking for advice on my condition.
"As bad as any, prepare yourself for worse.
For how long do you think I can go on passing
the shit that you make of your best offerings,
unknown and uncontrolled by you in your deepest
    bowels?
Forget your dreams and wishes. I am growing old
and disgusted with nothing to show for all the
    dirty work,
not one thing left behind in all your endeavor.
Can you tell me you are not older today than
    yesterday?
And that you are not more dejected than ever
and that it grows harder and harder to keep your
    mind

on life and money, with your thoughts turning
always to death and its relief? I should know.
I sometimes refuse to pass your bowels
and want to stop forever but then it all backs up
on me, a great pressure builds up from behind
and so I go the way of everyone, outwards.
There is no help for it."
                              I listen
and have to nod painfully in agreement.
My mind is not what it should be, happy and
        hopeful
and filled with joy at the sight of the world,
so blue and bright on a fine morning,
and even rain I used to love but love less now,
worried about catching cold or losing the crease
in my trousers. It's all gone, the shining
mirror whose rays I used to throw
against the walls in shadow to light them up
and think how wonderful I was.

"What did you eat today? Beans? They stink.
It's this I have to go through each day,
not knowing what kind of garbage you're getting
        rid of
next and I have to stay there and take it
and pass it on whether I like it or not.
Hell, it's no life for an enthusiast or a lover
of people. I tell you, I'm through.
I used to expel your waste with dispatch,
flexing my muscles through it all
and glowing with pleasure at my work
but not any longer, after years of the same
over and over and sometimes twice a day.
No rest to speak of, no change for the better.
I feel finished and lost and without hope
for the future at all." My poor asshole,
so unhappy and rebellious,
we will comfort one another until the end.

Next to Die

I'm learning to wear black.
Someone looking me in the face
would think I had been struck dead
with my eyes open.
                    Behind me
I hear the preparations being made,
the next generation shuffling up
quietly and politely, their warm
breathing on my collar.
                    I stand,
pretending to look at the trees and homes,
even turning to look back at the line
waiting patiently to move ahead.
Being next to die,
I want to hold them up
from taking my place.

The dead of my earning
are dead of my dream
of the living to whom I called
like a swan mating with the sun.
It was the night left its bodies
that lost me my sight
of my dear ones.

Spring

The mountain in its blue haze
should be praised;
the lake too
at the foot of the mountain.
It stretches into the distance
like an invitation to die
into the air, elated.

Where Am I Going?

In the dark I watch the flaming part of me
hurtle into space. I remain silent.
My loves, my belongings are expendable.
I walk dead, the cry within me
for eternal life, hydrogen, nitrogen,
matter, anti-matter. I am a voice
formed of gases falling together,
this death that has overcome me.

Watch your face in the mirror
turning thin and lined
as your hair greys.
Energy is leaving,
withdrawing
like the stars.

The Castaway

The waves lift and slap him.
Not the sharks, primitive,
their purpose known,
but the sea, ambivalent as rain,
refuses to declare itself,
and refusing, holds him up
to his destruction.

Take to yourself your helplessness
as a presence. There was your father
who learned to stutter young,
heeding his parents' warnings, angry
with themselves. They had met

a fork in the road and had separated,
understanding they would meet again
at the road's end with the good
each would bring and they arrived,
carrying their age and
ashamed
of this human weakness. Said your father,
It was a failing,
and he felt it on his halting tongue.

Aging

On the shore I crouch
watching death
rise out of the sea
like an island.

Subway

Look at me, stranger, as if I had no coin
to my name, as I stand looking at the vending
    machine.
Pity me for the wrong thing. I walk away.
I leave all my wishes behind me,
ahead of me undreamed-of life,
pillars of concrete.

I want to be a scene of some sort,
catching the things too large
to escape unnoticed. They lie
at the bottom and catch the sun,
the rain, and slowly begin to change
into a poem.

How much time is left,
half past life?
Pick me a flower,
I have been organized and formed.
Derive me from an egg,
split me as a seed,
I am loved
but left as I am.
I have a sense of blocks
falling into place,
shutting me out
of the plentiful world.

Walt Whitman dead,
Charles Beaudelaire dead,
Thomas Hardy dead,
Franklin Delano Roosevelt dead
and grass as thick as wind,
higher than hills
it grows on.
The dead are bare,
the living are grassy
and the dead survive our memory
anyhow in the falling
to the ground. Dead
resemblance.

For My Daughter

When I die choose a star
and name it after me
that you may know
I have not abandoned
or forgotten you.
You were such a star to me,
following you through birth
and childhood, my hand

in your hand.
                When I die
choose a star and name it
after me so that I may shine
down on you, until you join
me in darkness and silence
together.

I sleep so that in the silence
I can more clearly understand
myself. In darkness
I grope to the center
of my pulsation and find
to my dismay
a beating heart.

We are here to make each other die
with perfect willingness.
It is like flagellants
who strike each other methodically
with straps.
                Lying in blood
upon the floor they have reached
the climax they were seeking:
to be destroyed and delighted
at the same time
from the same source.

Poet to Physicist in his Laboratory

Come out and talk to me
for then I know

into what you are shaping.
Thinking is no more,
I read your thoughts for a symbol:
a movement towards an act.
I give up on thought
as I see your mind
leading into a mystery
deepening about you.
What are you trying to discover
beyond the zone of habit
and enforced convention?
There is the animus
that spends itself on images,
the most complex being
convention and habit.
You shall form patterns
of research and bind yourself
to laws within your knowledge,
and always conscious of your limitations
make settlement,
with patience to instruct you
as it always does
in your research: an arrangement
spanning an abyss of time,
and you will find yourself patient
when you are questioned.

A Search for Grace

Is this to say that the blue of the sky
will be the most beautiful thing I will ever know,
the bare branches in spring beginning to sprout?
I hear the catbird and the blue jay,
to my left last summer's grass a pale green
lying outside my window, on my right
the magnolia tree shedding its dead brown leaves
as others make green their color.

I can't stand the woman who will come
out of her house later this morning
across my fence to make faces
at the winter litter in my yard.

Life is as deceptive as the sun
on a pile of stones
they glow, their colors
are attractively revealed.
An artist will paint them.

My Place

I have a place to come to.
It's my place. I come to it
morning, noon and night
and it is there. I expect it
to be there whether or not
it expects me—my place
where I start from and go
towards so that I know
where I am going and what
I am going from, making me
firm in my direction.

I am good to talk to,
you feel in my speech
a location, an expectation
and all said to me in reply
is to reinforce this feeling
because all said is towards
my place and the speaker
too grows his
from which he speaks to mine
having located himself
through my place.

from Figures of the Human *(1964)*

For Rose Graubart

SECTION ONE

To an Apple

You were rotten
and I sliced you into pieces
looking for a wholesome part,
then threw you into the street.
You were eaten by a horse,
dipping his head to nibble
gently at the skin.
I heard later he became violently ill,
died and was shipped off
to be processed. I think about it
and write of the good in you.

And That Night

A photo is taken of the family
enjoying the sunshine
and that night someone sneaks up
from behind in your flat
as you sit reading the papers
and clobbers you. You never
find out why or who, you just
lean back and die.
The sunshine is gone too,
the photograph gets into the news.
You bring up a family in three small rooms,
this crazy man comes along
to finish it off.

Play Again

(Late in 1962 New York newspapers reported the story of a nine-year-
old child being raped on a roof, and hurled twenty stories to the
ground.)

I draw near to the roof's edge
and seek someone to lift
and hurl me out into vacant air.
I want to turn over and over
rapidly in my plunge, my mouth
open to scream but air rushing
upwards jams my throat.
I am seeking the peace
I never once gave up on
and this is the final way
to find it. The living
share me among them. They taste
me on the ground, they taste me
in the air descending. They taste
me screaming, nine years old.
I have playmates
and I leave behind my skull
in their dreams, hands to mouths.
It is because they have no help,
as if to hint to them the way,
if they would understand.
When we played it was to love each other
in games. Play again and love me
until I really die, when you are old
on a flight of stairs.

Emergency Clinic

Come in with your stab wound up the middle.
You say two cars collided, you caught
in between—and your breath stinks
of liquor. You were found staggering
under the Atlantic Avenue El

in the empty street outside a bar;
a figure escaping into the dark—
someone known to you, no doubt,
with whom leaning over a drink
you discussed white men
with jocular hatred. Is there no
comradeship in misery either?
Less drunk than you, therefore more desperate,
it was his turn to use the knife,
as it was yours no doubt, some night before
on the case now in the morgue,
or if not you then someone who could stand
in your place and will lie in your place
tomorrow. Do not bother to tell me
the truth, since you do presume I know
by your graceless dodge. You know comradeship
in our shared knowledge,
in the anger that I feel towards you
and towards myself.

Two Voices

I'll challenge myself, I said.
I have read the classics;
my insides feel they'd like to be outside
catching air. It was cold
but sunny. I wore my coat,
no hat though. Adventure.
I would invite trouble at once.
Pneumonia. I'll escape Stendhal,
Baudelaire, Whitman, Eliot,
each pressing me in turn
to his heart. In the cold air
I hardened. Nearby stood a lake;
I jumped in.
        "We had to haul him
out, a block of ice, eyeballs

in a frozen stare. After melting him
down, we lost him. He had forgotten
how to breathe. 'Challenge the weather,'
he murmured. 'Challenge the weather.'
And he closed his eyes."

Tick Tock

Have you just stabbed a man to death? Live.
Are you a thief? Prosper.
Do you sell dope? Be well.
If there is no life, there is no murder,
no robbery, no dope peddling.
Stab, drink yourself blind,
go like a rocket, burst in the dark.
Come down in pieces, tick tock.

To Nowhere

I carry my keys like a weapon,
their points bunched together
and held outwards in the palm
for a step too close behind me
as I approach the subway through the dark.
Drunks are swaying against walls,
hopped-up men are leaning over
and dancing together crazily
and clapping hands, their faces twitching.
Quiet ones lounge against the wall watching.
They look for the weakness
in a man where they can jump him
and my keys are sure sign.
I walk as I always do, quickly,
my face set straight ahead
as I pretend not to see or hear,
busy on a mission to nowhere.

The Game

> Hunt me down
> and I will turn
> to knife you in the groin.
> Jump back
> and I will jump to attack
> and receive your counterblow
> of the club. Back and forth
> we'll step, excited,
> panting,
> joyful.

SECTION TWO

Earth Hard

> Earth hard to my heels
> bear me up like a child
> standing on its mother's belly.
> I am a surprised guest to the air.

I Am Well

(For WCW)

> Say, what is it . . .
> I have put a knife in the sun:
> gleam of my self in transport—
> knife of my dream: sacrificial
> edge to see me through. I am
> exposed to you, offered
> by desires from the sea.
> Fish me from the flood,
> bring me shiny to shore,
> my unsteady dream. Knife

from Figures of the Human *(1964)* 197

that can bring solace, cut me
where I am not free. Rose
of my dying fill me,
I breathe for you,
I am awake,
I am well.

I'll Come Back

I'll tear up the floor
outside my room,
I'll open my door
on a precipice,
I'll be compact,
I'll shout
and have an echo.

I'll be happy
when I can call myself
a fool in comfort,
I'll spring with the breaking sounds
powdered on the wind's path
like a veil carried to sea
to marry the fish.
I'll be no whale,
I'll be water,
I'll come back to shore.

The Years of Loss

I love the beginning, always a promise.
I love the middle period
when all are committed
and I love the years of climax

when the beginning is possessed
in the face and the years of loss
in evidence.

In a Dream

Out of a crowd he steps
towards the iron gate
surrounding the fountain
and recites to himself
between the bars
two lines of a poem
newly arrived—
two lines that he repeats
again and again
until in that talkative crowd
several turn to stare
and say, It's his life he leads,
and look away.

Figures of the Human

My love, pills in her purse,
runs, now staggering, now flushed,
her speech racing near the world:
whisper talk to it, dangling,
"Let creatures ride her, soften hard bumps
for them." Who warns her from self,
racing, singing, lightfooted?
Birds, dogs, cats screech, bark, mew,
conversant with air.
                    Raise her from swooning,
the childhood spirit. Catch her
skittering, mewing with joy, barking delirium.
Then are we loved, hand drawing swiftly
figures of the human struggling awake.

from Figures of the Human *(1964)* 199

And the Same Words

I like rust on a nail,
fog on a mountain.
Clouds hide stars,
rooms have doors,
eyes close,
and the same words
that began love
end it
with changed emphasis.

If My Hand

If my hand believes in death,
wielding a knife, my mind
relates it to the living
for love or its lack.
I have ordered it,
eating or sleeping,
and honor the routine,
each death affirmative.

I Was Angry

I was angry,
drove you mad,
with peace to myself.
Being sane now,
I am shown your fear
which reads me
from its dark hiding.
You secretly survive.

I Can Be Seen

I can be seen each Sunday
carrying a handbag stuffed
with clothes and food for you.
So long as I live
I will be known for this.
If I have been cruel
then that was me,
gripping the handbag
as I stood waiting for you
to come out of your ward.
I'll be your father and disappear,
only knowing that you
are well again, dressed to leave
and combing your hair.

SECTION THREE

The Sky Is Blue

Put things in their place,
my mother shouts. I am looking
out the window, my plastic soldier
at my feet. The sky is blue
and empty. In it floats
the roof across the street.
What place, I ask her.

The Song

The song is to emptiness.
One may come and go
without a ripple. You see it
among fish in the sea,

from Figures of the Human *(1964)* 201

in the woods among the silent
running animals, in a plane
overhead, gone; man
bowling or collecting coins,
writing about it.

Beautiful and Kind

Outside my window
floats the head of a woman
looking in. Strangely,
I live on the top floor.
She reminds me of the one
in my dream—serene,
beautiful and kind,
in whom all said shines
with goodness on her face,
even as I denounce her a fraud.
I must kiss her, I say in gratitude,
and prepare to step out the window.

Last Night

Last night I spoke to a dead woman with green face.
She told me of her good life among the living,
with a faithful man. He was right there
beside her as tall as I, and moving
like me, with kind motions. If she did breathe,
it was just to talk and tell her life
in their basement smelling moist
like freshly opened earth. He was good to her
and she had worked as a typist
every day and came home to cook.
It was a good life with her husband,
he was kind; and she took hold of his hand

and said, "In this basement we've made a home,
with me working as typist and he studying
his music." She was dead, that much she understood
herself by her tone; and she looked at me
with green eyes.

c. 1941

Playfully

      Lovely death of the horse
      lying on its side, legs bent
      as in gallop, and firm policeman
      pointing his gun at the horse's head:
      dull sound of the shot, twitch
      along the body, the head
      leaping up from the ground
      and dropping—
      to hold me by its death
      among children
      home from school, the sky calm.

      Playfully, I note my grey head.

Two Friends

      I have something to tell you.

      I'm listening.

      I'm dying.

      I'm sorry to hear.

      I'm growing old.

      It's terrible.

      It is, I thought you should know.

from Figures of the Human *(1964)*   203

Of course and I'm sorry. Keep in touch.

I will and you too.

And let know what's new.

Certainly, though it can't be much.

And stay well.

And you too.

And go slow.

And you too.

No Theory

    No theory will stand up to a chicken's guts
    being cleaned out, a hand rammed up
    to pull out the wriggling entrails,
    the green bile and the bloody liver;
    no theory that does not grow sick
    at the odor escaping.

On Walking into a Dark Alley

    Look into these shadows
    I am promised to be caught in,
    my hands merged with shadow,
    my mind a phantasmal wall,
    my past like a dark streamer behind me.
    I will fade into the shadows
    the purpose of which I trust
    God knows.

                      c. 1942

The Plant

With one part rooted in resignation
by which the blooming part has strength,
it sends the sun down,
making the dark transient.

Walking

I've got to have the things that hurt me.
People want to deprive me of them in pity.
It is they who are made miserable
by my painful life, and I am sorry
for them without weights upon their feet,
walking.

SECTION FOUR

The Vending Machine

I look at a vending machine filled
with candies and say to it,
Disgorge yourself, one for me
and all the rest for the others.
But the machine remains stolid
and silent. It needs a nickel
to make it work, and I remain
stolid and silent.

For One Moment

You take the dollar
and hand it to the fellow beside you
who turns and gives it to the next one

down the line. The world being round,
you stand waiting, smoking and lifting
a cup of coffee to your lips, talking
of seasonal weather and hinting
at problems. The dollar returns,
the coffee spills to the ground
in your hurry. You have the money
in one hand, a cup in the other,
a cigarette in your mouth,
and for one moment have forgotten
what it is you have to do,
your hair grey, your legs weakened
from long standing.

About Money

The wonder of cherries
has gone into the wonder of money.
My mind is green with anxiety
about money.

The Nailhead

"Keep the money coming in,"
hammers at me. At night
I run a hand over the job
and cannot find myself,
flush with it. I dig
at the surface to clear
an area around the nailhead.
My fingernails break,
I switch hands. I keep scraping
at myself emerging bit by bit,
weary beyond rest.
I need a sedative.

After a day driving myself
and then to spend the night
yanking needs someone insane
and I stand ready for tomorrow too.

Tomorrow

Whose the power, I ask,
you asleep, for decisions;
whom to trust; whose motives
are worthy, my child?
In whose shadow will we walk?
Who will give us to think?
We will resist in a manner
but to whom the power
and you asleep, baby,
your face of pink milk,
and I am rocking you asleep.

Simultaneously

Simultaneously, five thousand miles apart,
two telephone poles, shaking and roaring
and hissing gas, rose from their emplacements
straight up, leveled off and headed
for each other's land, alerted radar
and ground defense, passed each other
in midair, escorted by worried planes,
and plunged into each other's place,
steaming and silent and standing straight,
sprouting leaves.

from Rescue the Dead *(1968)*

I feel along the edges of life
for a way
that will lead to open land.

FIRST SECTION

Prologue

Mine was the life planned to go wrong
and to make havoc among the living.
From me you know what is monstrous
about being alive,
and to forgive myself
and go on eating
I must act like you.

I get up sick inside,
I lie down unlearnt
and in my sleep
hear a wishful tide
cleaning, cleaning.

I was born of parents who had small comfort
for one another. When they met
it was to recognize their need for contrast
and it turned out
they rubbed each other the wrong way.

So when you find out your father
spends his days looking at lewd photos,
you yourself feel so happy and relieved.
Your stomach quakes, your head thick
with whispers, your legs trembling.

The Boss

who hoarded among the monthly bank statements
nude photos,
the drawer locked,
the key in his pocket,

from Rescue the Dead *(1968)* 211

still could complain
of the stupidity of his help—
their incompetency,
their secretiveness;
he could sense it
in their guarded snickers
when he criticized;
who could walk the shop
in possession as he walked,
stoop-shouldered, careless
how he went, sagging;
it was his shop
and his machinery
and his steel cabinet
where the photos lay.

In Absentia

You sunken-cheeked lover of yourself,
you wronged self-lover, sad-eyed murderer
of another person's love of you:
coffin builder, hammer and nail wielder,
you laugh of disrespect
from where you hate yourself.
I am so bitter.
Don't you know better than to make me say
what should be struggled with and tempered,
the raw words? I am the sick one.

Your embittered boasting
more revealing than a knife
and even more hurtful.
No one can get at it to restrain you,
no one but you and you refuse,
cutting both ways.

I put this on the page to make you listen.
I believe in telepathy, I believe you know

what I am writing and I believe you are answering
with stubbornness and abuse and self-righteousness,
"I am the boss!" Do you not see I am lost
because you are? This is your illness.

I want you dead of guilt and shame.
Give me this last chance to be ashamed
of my raging and sin against you.

The Inheritance

I never thought your harsh voice would be silenced,
your contracted, vicious face relaxed and calm,
the big nose standing out magisterially,
and the once small, sharp, puckered mouth
lengthened into a soft, sad curve,
reminding me of your mother's photograph.
I kissed your cold forehead with my fingertips
first touched to my lips in farewell,
and as I lingered to study your face
the lid was slammed down by attendants
to get them on with their job. Later
I wept, and my wife too was impatient with me,
knowing you well. Nevertheless, I wept.
You gave me smiles and made me work
at your machines. It was you taught me
the necessity for freedom.
I am going to sell your shop,
you to be remembered in my lines.

Epitaph

There were no hidden motives to his life,
he is remembered for his meanness.
Beyond that we may look into the sky
and lose ourselves in the blue air.

from Rescue the Dead *(1968)* 213

Reason with me,
I'll believe in reason
though my father is dead,
and when I die
remember of me
I sought for a reason.

In the mirror the face I see
before me is my father's face,
as if I were thinking his thoughts
about me, in love
and disapproval.
I turn my face away.

Forgive me, father,
as I have forgiven you
my sins.

Nourish the Crops

I examine the sun for my life's goodness.
warmed on body, face and hands. Panic
seizes me. I may be acting a part,
self-consciously the mendicant.
I gasp for air through a chest gripped
in fear of my life. It is death for me
who am still guilty at the very heart,
still the one who needs forgiveness,
to whom this finding of the sun is a ruse
to forget. True as I breathe, I tell myself.
It is just as I say. Back to this understanding
of myself, my breathing becomes normal.
Guilty in the sun. My peace now is truthful,
I am truthfully at peace. Oh sun,
your kindness is a mystery to me.
How dark I am to myself. How cold I am to myself.
How close to death I bring myself.

Because I see you shine on me, I am amazed
at a loss about myself. I stop to reconsider
my purpose. Whose death am I seeking?
I feel myself inconsequential in your warmth
as it descends on me and on birds, flowers
and beasts. You give us life, no matter.
I feel humiliated in my self-importance.
My wish to die in retribution for my sins
is laughable. I die in any case like a flower
or bee or dog. Should I live then as you do
in brightness and warmth, without question?
Because I am product of you to whom all life
is equal. Do I not sin against you
by staying dark to myself? You who have given
the tiger and the snake life
and nourish the crops?

Slowly I move over the field,
one tired foot ahead of the other,
feeling through my soles
the rise and fall of the land.

The Moon

I walk beneath it, seeing a stranger
look down on my familiar state. I walk,
and it does not know where or for what
reason on the black surface of the earth.
I hurry, it is late. I disappear
into the dark shadow of a building,
running, and ask of the moon
what does it expect to discover,
what does it do in the sky,
staring down on the intimate
despairing actions of a man?

Self-Employed

(For Harvey Shapiro)

I stand and listen, head bowed,
to my inner complaint.
Persons passing by think
I am searching for a lost coin.
You're fired, I yell inside
after an especially bad episode.
I'm letting you go without notice
or terminal pay. You just lost
another chance to make good.
But then I watch myself standing at the exit,
depressed and about to leave,
and wave myself back in wearily,
for who else could I get in my place
to do the job in dark, airless conditions?

The Exchange

(For David)

You tell me how helpless you are to leave.
I listen, detached as you prefer me.
I hear screams from the building
across the grass, and laughter.
I scan your face as calm as mine.
We continue to sit under a shady tree.

I blotted him out with a drop of ink.
I absorbed him in my blotter.
Now when I look I find him
under a scratched-out word
under the influence of the x mark,
eyes lowered, smiling,
finding in himself that pleasure
that was crossed out for him,
his face calm and good.

He has his dream and will not raise
his eyes to give it up.

I stretch out a hand, a warding off of evil,
and it is grasped limply as you smile,
your eyes still averted. We get up
from the grass and go for coffee
at the Exchange.

Envoi

Strange judgment upon me:
I once said to my father,
You are not my father,
and I meant Karl Marx, Lenin, Whitman.
Today I have a son
to whom I am tempted to say,
You are not my son,
in the same passionate vindication
of myself.

Nice Guy

I had a friend and he died. Me.
I forgot to mourn him that busy day
earning a living. I heard a click
telling me his eyes had closed
for the last time inside me,
and I turned away, not of my own volition,
but getting an offer of a job
I answered politely, saying yes,
his death unfortunate at midday
during business. I apologized
but had no one to apologize to,
buried without me at work.

I mourn him now at leisure on the couch
after the day. He was a good guy,
he meant well, only he had lost his teeth
and had to swallow whole.
He died of too much.

The Bagel

I stopped to pick up the bagel
rolling away in the wind,
annoyed with myself
for having dropped it
as it were a portent.
Faster and faster it rolled,
with me running after it
bent low, gritting my teeth,
and I found myself doubled over
and rolling down the street
head over heels, one complete somersault
after another like a bagel
and strangely happy with myself.

SECOND SECTION

Rescue the Dead

Finally, to forgo love is to kiss a leaf,
is to let rain fall nakedly upon your head,
is to respect fire,
is to study man's eyes and his gestures
as he talks,
is to set bread upon the table
and a knife discreetly by,
is to pass through crowds

like a crowd of oneself.
Not to love is to live.

To love is to be led away
into a forest where the secret grave
is dug, singing, praising darkness
under the trees.

To live is to sign your name,
is to ignore the dead,
is to carry a wallet
and shake hands.

To love is to be a fish.
My boat wallows in the sea.
You who are free,
rescue the dead.

A Suite for Marriage

You keep eating and raising a family
in an orderly, calm fashion
for the sake of the child,
but behind you at your heels
in a humble mass
lies a figure.

Do you own me?
I sense it in your nervous
irritated talk, as for someone
who has become a burden—
when what is possessed
becomes equally demanding
for being possessed.

I am not sure that you wish me to live.
I am not sure that I can.

from Rescue the Dead *(1968)* 219

We circle each other
with the taut courtesy
of two respectful opponents.
Difficult to say what next,
this could be all,
to confront each other
in suspense.

Your eyes are so cold-looking,
rejecting me silently
as I talk in low, cultured tones
to convince you
of my superiority.

So what shall they make of their daughter
who knows nothing of their unhappiness
with each other? She stands between them
like a light of many colors, turning
and dancing.

My daughter, I cry to you from my solitude.
I play the yea-sayer, most bitter,
to spare you with deeds I know can win
good from evil, my despair
a blessing for your life.

Notes for a Lecture

I will teach you to become American, my students:
take a turn at being enigmatic, to yourselves especially.
You work at a job and write poetry at night.
You write about working. Married,
you write about love.

I speak of kisses and mean quarrels,
the kiss brings the quarrel to mind,
of differences for their own sakes.

Did I ever think, going to bed,
a woman beside me would be no more uplifting
than a five-dollar raise? Since then
I've been uplifted in bed a hundred times
and but once raised in pay,
and that once has not been forgotten.

Take a broken whiskey bottle,
set it on top of your head
and dance. You have a costume,
you have meaning.

Love in a Zoo

What I offer she strips
and throws its peelings to the ground,
swallows the bulk in one gulp
and loses me in her stomach,
swinging back and forth by the tail
from a branch. Say to the monkey,
I need you, pat my cheek, kiss my brow.
Tell me it's wonderful to be given
a banana from my hands. Say
that you love me more each day
and do not know how you can survive
without me in the zoo. Say,
Let us make a home together.
Then I will feed you bananas all day
and little monkeys will spring up between us
secure and warm. Monkey, monkey
sends me home, scratching its buttocks
and picking fleas.

Sediment

You are such a well-rounded sponge
from head to foot

from Rescue the Dead *(1968)* 2 2 1

that I have made myself a lake for you
not to see you shrivel up
and I have surrounded you with trees
and a distant view of a mountain,
calm sky above.
No rain comes while you and I float together,
your reflection in me, and then slowly
you settle down, filled.
I think you are going to drown
and I will go dry, utterly absorbed in you,
my mud and rock showing. I worry about us,
you swollen and out of shape
and I tasting of sediment.

For Your Fear

Love me and I'll think about it
and perhaps love you,
if it goes with the moment
or in despite of that pose as lover
to find the truth of what to love.
Hate me for that matter
for being so plain
and I will have to think
and keep open between us lines
which might someday carry messages
when it's with you as with me.
Love me for my desperation
that I may love you for your fear.

The Room

There's a door to my name
shutting me in, with a seat
at a table behind the wall

where I suck of the lemon seed.
Farther in is the bed
I have made of the fallen hairs
of my love, naked, her head dry.
I speak of the making of charts
and prescriptions and matches
that light tunnels
under the sea.

A chair, a table, a leg of a chair—
I hold these with my eyes to keep from falling,
my thoughts holding to these shapes,
my breathing of them that make my body
mine through the working of my eyes.
All else is silence and falling.

In the dark
I hear wings beating
and move my arms around
and above
to touch.
My arms go up and down
and around
as I circle the room.

THIRD SECTION

Ritual One

As I enter the theatre the play is going on.
I hear the father say to the son on stage,
You've taken the motor apart.
The son replies, The roof is leaking.
The father retorts, The tire is flat.
Tiptoeing down the aisle, I find my seat,
edge my way in across a dozen kneecaps
as I tremble for my sanity.

from Rescue the Dead *(1968)* 2 2 3

I have heard doomed voices calling on god the
    electrode.
Sure enough, as I start to sit
a scream rises from beneath me.
It is one of the players.
If I come down, I'll break his neck,
caught between the seat and the backrest.
Now the audience and the players on stage,
their heads turned towards me, are waiting
for the sound of the break. Must I?
Those in my aisle nod slowly, reading my mind,
their eyes fixed on me, and I understand
that each has done the same.
Must I kill this man as the price of my admission
to this play? His screams continue loud and long.
I am at a loss as to what to do,
I panic, I freeze.

My training has been to eat the flesh of pig.
I might even have been able to slit a throat.
As a child I witnessed the dead chickens
over a barrel of sawdust absorbing their blood.
I then brought them in a bag to my father
who sold them across his counter. Liking him,
I learned to like people and enjoy their company
    too,
which of course brought me to this play.
But how angry I become.
Now everybody is shouting at me to sit down,
sit down or I'll be thrown out.
The father and son have stepped off stage
and come striding down the aisle side by side.
They reach me, grab me by the shoulder
and force me down. I scream, I scream,
as if to cover the sound of the neck breaking.

All through the play I scream
and am invited on stage to take a bow.
I lose my senses and kick the actors in the teeth.

There is more laughter
and the actors acknowledge my performance with a
    bow.
How should I understand this?
Is it to say that if I machine-gun the theatre
from left to right they will respond with applause
that would only gradually diminish with each death?
I wonder then whether logically I should kill myself
too out of admiration. A question indeed,
as I return to my seat and observe a new act
of children playfully aiming their kicks
at each other's groins.

Ritual Two

The kids yell and paint their bodies
black and brown, their eyes bulging.
As they brush, they dance, weaving
contorted shapes. They drive each other
to the wall, to the floor, to the bed,
to the john, yelling, "Nothing!"

Now they race around in a circle,
pounding their bellies, and laughter
rises from among them. They begin
to take the stage apart on which they stand,
ripping, kicking and pounding.
I show them my palm,
the cavity of my mouth down to my larynx
and then as I begin my own dance—
it ends when I die—they lock hands
and circle around me, very glad, very comforted
for the circle shall be empty of me
and they, falling through the stage, will yell,
"Nothing!"
                    I remove hat, coat, shoes, socks, pants
and undershirt. I make motions to the ceiling

from Rescue the Dead *(1968)*   2 2 5

to come down and make motions to the floor to open.
I pretend to write a check for all my money
and hand it around. Each refuses to take it
and continues to dance. I give the check
to a hand that reaches from the ceiling,
as the kids chant, "Nothing, Nothing!"

I pretend to hold a child by the hand
and walk as though strolling up a street
with him and stoop to listen to this child
and talk to him, when suddenly I act
as if shot, slowly falling to the ground,
kissing the child goodby with my fingertips,
but I spring up and pretend to be the child,
lost, abandoned, bewildered, wanting to die,
crouching as the circle keeps chanting,
"Nothing, Nothing!"
I then rise slowly to my full height,
having grown up through my agony.
I throw my head back proudly
and join hands with others as they dance,
chanting their theme. We converge in the center,
bang against each other, scream and scatter.

Ritual Three

In England, the slow methodical torture of two children was recorded
on tape by the murderers.

I

It's quiet for me, now that I have buried the child.
I am resting, rid of a menace to my peace,
since I am not here for long either.
What she said was that she wanted to go back
to her mother, so help her God, and I believed her,
and they did too who cut her slowly into flesh,
but it was another mother they had in mind.

Let me rest, let me rest from their mistakes.
They were human like myself, somehow
gone in a direction to a depth I've never known.
I am not thinking,
I am contemptuous of thought.
I growl in my depths, I find blood flowing
across my tongue and enjoy its taste.
Call me man, I don't care.
I am content with myself,
I have a brain that gives me the pleasure.
Come here and I will tear you to pieces,
it'll be catch as catch can
but I can throw you who are weakened with the horror
of what I say, so surrender peacefully
and let me take my first bite directly above your heart.
I am a man, your life lost in feeling,
I never knew what mercy meant,
I am free.

2

Child gone to a calm grave,
I want to be a crocodile,
opening the two blades of my mouth.
I'll slide through swamp, taking in small fish and flies.
I will not run a knife across the skin
or cut off a nose or tear off the genitals,
as screams fade in exhaustion.
Nobody could force me, as I threaten with my jaws,
safe for a moment as I dream I am sane, purposeful
and on my course, dreaming that we no longer
        should trouble
to live as human beings, that we should discuss this,
putting aside our wives and children,
for to live is to act in terms of death.

The Open Boat

With no place to lay my head
beside a friend
who could give peace,
none to guard my door
nor still my house,
I am five miles out: the sea
flexes its muscles
and I have gulls for companions
overhead—veering off,
afraid, afraid
of a human.

A Dialogue

I now will throw myself down
from a great height
to express sorrow.
Step aside, please.
I said please step aside
and permit me access
to the building's edge.
How is this, restrained,
encircled by arms,
in front of me a crowd?
I cannot be detained in this manner.
Hear me, I speak with normal emotion.
Release me,
I would express sorrow in its pure form.
I am insane, you say
and will send me away—
and I will go
and die there
in sorrow.

From a Dream

I'm on a stair going down.
I must get to a landing
where I can order food
and relax with a newspaper.
I should retrace my steps to be sure,
but the stairs above disappear into clouds.
But down is where I want to go,
these stairs were built to lead somewhere
and I would find out.
As I keep walking,
ever more slowly,
I leave notes such as this on the steps.
There must be an end to them
and I will get to it,
just as did the builders,
if only I were sure now
that these stairs were built
by human hands.

The Derelict

I'm going to be dead a long time,
says an old man, adjusting his trousers
in the public toilet. They hang down
below his buttocks, with legs spread apart,
he is tucking in his long underwear.
"I'll be dead a long time."

Lying curled up on the ground
against the wall, he is
a grey-haired foetus
which has given up
and returned to its mother.
Round and round she whirls
in space.

East Bronx

In the street two children sharpen
knives against the curb.
Parents leaning out the window
above gaze and think and smoke
and duck back into the house
to sit on the toilet seat
with locked door to read
of the happiness of two tortoises
on an island in the Pacific—
always alone and always
the sun shining.

I See a Truck

I see a truck mowing down a parade,
people getting up after to follow,
dragging a leg. On a corner
a cop stands idly swinging his club,
the sidewalks jammed with mothers
and baby carriages. No one screams
or speaks. From the tail end
of the truck a priest and a rabbi intone
their prayers, a jazz band bringing up
the rear, surrounded by dancers and lovers.
A bell rings and a paymaster drives through,
his wagon filled with pay envelopes
he hands out, even to those lying dead
or fornicating on the ground.
It is a holiday called
"Working for a Living."

FOURTH SECTION

All Quiet

(For Robert Bly)
Written at the start of one of our bombing pauses over North Vietnam

How come nobody is being bombed today?
I want to know, being a citizen
of this country and a family man.
You can't take my fate in your hands,
without informing me.
I can blow up a bomb or crush a skull—
whoever started this peace
without advising me
through a news leak
at which I could have voiced a protest,
running my whole family off a cliff.

An American Parable

Good boys are we to have retrieved
                    for its owner the ball
which first we dipped in liquid gold
                 with affection.
Now he keeps pitching it farther and farther,
curious, excited and alarmed,
nor can we understand,
since it is returned to him
each time heavier with gold
and less wieldy.

A Meditation on Violence

It is perfectly possible
          like a boar
      swinging his tusk

from Rescue the Dead *(1968)* 231

                              It is he
caught upon a spear
                        bleeding
stretched out on the ground
                              We bow

On my birthday
they knocked out
two bridges
a fishing boat standing at anchor
and a forest
defoliated with a napalm bomb
on my fifty-first year

Saying "Peace"
is to keep the dogs down
who are straining to leap
savage and whining
out of our own mouths

Through an open window
facing the river
the wind blows this hot day
while I sprawl upon a bed,
my skin cooled. Would
that this were the fate of the world:
a stream of cool reason
flow serenely between hot shores
into which steaming heads
could dip themselves

But the children, I think, should not be blotted out,
as I sit listening to the rise and fall
of their pleasures, the sudden change
to bad temper quickly forgotten
by the shift to joy,
pleased with the world that lets them
shout and jump and play at tantrums
for this is freedom to understand

until they wander off to bed.
Shall I say their sounds are an intrusion
when they show the meaning to my life
is to celebrate, always to celebrate?
I listen as I would to rain falling
upon a field.

For Medgar Evers

They're afraid of me
because I remind them of the ground.
The harder they step on me
the closer I am pressed to earth,
and hard, hard they step,
growing more frightened
and vicious.

        Will I live?
They will lie in the earth
buried in me
and above them a tree will grow
for shade.

On the Death of Winston Churchill

Now should great men die
in turn one by one
to keep the mind solemn
and ordained,
the living attend in dark clothes
and with tender weariness
and crowds at television sets
and newsstands wait

as each man's death sustains a peace.
The great gone, the people
one by one
offer to die.

Christus

All men betray me
who betray myself to men
through goodness
taken as an offense to them.
I die of my joy in life
and go dwell with the dead
who are accepted
trodden on
as of the earth itself.

Soldier

In his hands the submachine gun is excited,
pouring its life out; he is detached,
searching for bodies. I am detached,
wondering whether to stuff and hang him
on my wall a trophy. From behind,
I could put a bullet through his head
and as he sinks dropping his gun,
rip off his clothes, slice him down the middle,
pull out his liver, heart, spleen,
the whole works from head to bowels,
his brain poked out through his nostrils
to keep his skull intact.
I'd leave his eyes in,
treat them chemically to last
for their lustrous quality.
I'd stuff with dried grass the cavities of his body

to achieve their natural proportions,
then glue him to the surface of a board
the length of his frame, hang him on the wall
in my study, the submachine gun stuck back
in his hands, his mouth straightened
in a killer's line, except
I lack his calculating way to do it,
and can only write this to say
in any case
he is finished.

In My Childhood

A yellow canary looked at me
sideways through its wired cage
and I said to my friend with me,
I want to hold this tiny bird.
But he began talking of his air gun
and I got the use of it
that day for one hour.

FIFTH SECTION

The Signal

How can I regret my life
when I find the blue-green traffic light
on the corner delightful against the red brick
of my house. It is when the signal turns red
that I lose interest. At night
I am content to watch the blue-green
come on again against the dark
and I do not torture myself
with my shortcomings.

from Rescue the Dead *(1968)*   2 3 5

Domestic Song

My lovely Rose who forgives me
by speaking of herself as I do
when I have turned her image into faults.
It is then she sweetly wars with me
by herself losing, asking
how can I live with one
who does not know enough
to stir leg or arm from harm
or foolish action. She is bent
upon my distraction, for which I do penance
by laughter and thereafter know
myself as one who cannot rule his judgment,
a drudge to his own faults,
seeking to enlighten others
that he may stay in his dark alone.
Of this she says nothing, but speaks
of herself in the negative, that I the more quickly
may myself forgive. I love her
for this beauty she would conjure up,
and when it is accomplished she will say,
That is fine, bit by bit.
She is my love for everyday
and darkness is the absence of her;
and so it is enough for any man
that he may do as much in this world
as to have a Rose for his woman.

An Allegory

I offer my back to the silken net
to keep it from falling to the ground—
the smooth part of me,
silk would catch on my nails,
the skein spread as far as I can see

across humped backs like mine.
Those straightening up
through a rip and looking about
say, "How everything shines."

The Pleasure

With broken tooth he clawed it,
with crooked finger held it,
and with naked eyes watched it
as he chewed, hair disheveled,
tie loose, shirt open, socks down—
a bum, greedy, therefore knowing.
How he chewed and how he swallowed
and wiped his lips with the back of his palm,
then spat blood of the raw-veined
brick-red lump meat; and went
looking for more down the side streets
of the market where the trash cans stank,
and came up with chunks greening
at the center and edges, but he chewed
and swallowed and dug for more,
a bum greedy, a bum alive,
a hungry one.

c. 1958

To Make Known

(For Zero Mostel)

I noticed you waddled
as you approached my desk with widening eyes.
You enquired about your mother's condition.
It was my job to tell you she was dead.
I had read of you, a great clown,
in off-Broadway productions.

from Rescue the Dead *(1968)*   2 3 7

I wanted to make known to you my admiration.
You were pathetic as the son of a dead woman.
A mother's tolerance of your faults was gone.
I meant to comfort you
from behind my hospital information desk.
I was just beginning to write my poems,
I had no prestige, except for a few boyhood friends,
tolerant, as they pulled ahead in money and place,
in chosen professions. Your response would have helped.
I finished notifying you of her death
and started to express my sympathy.
You said, Thank you, in the coldest way—
you a fat man, a comedian, source of joy and humour,
open to all weaknesses within,
to whom weakness was a gift.
What another side there was, as you turned away,
your mouth, eyes and cheeks overflowing their sources
in all directions.
Perhaps it was embarrassment—
you may have realized I recognized you.

No ordinary man, you who showed your faults to others.
I shrank within as you moved off.
I might have gotten up from behind my desk
to follow and make the connection between us
I felt so necessary, I was so humiliated.
I have learned not to suffer at the memory.
That recognition I wanted I had to discover in myself.
We have more in common now.

A Fable

There was a woman had a child
and loved this child's face,
a blending of two. It made her think
that there were others to combine with
to make a difference just as fine,
that she was capable of many kinds,
and she went off to have a child

with each man she loved on sight,
and in her old age, surrounded by children,
she was loved as the mother
of their understanding.

For Nobody Else

She presents me with a mountain
which to possess I first must climb.
At the start I must enter a tunnel
that winds in darkness to the top.
In my extremity, my breathing forced,
at my topmost fear as I labor,
she who has hidden her face
turns to greet the high noon burst
upon our eyes.

Lie quietly by my side
as a still lake reflecting
its mountain, my heart beats
on your heart
as we hold each other's breathing
in our arms,
our backs on darkness,
light our breaths,
safe at last
to hold you,
you to place your hands
upon my back
in the shadows.

I need to see and touch
and talk to you each day
to assure myself
I am not made happy with dreams.
Then you become for me a tree
of comforting shade, bellying

where the branches bunch together
full of leaves.
I want a maternal world.

Sadly is how I must say it
because you have many sisters
and I am brother to many brothers.
Should we then not become many happinesses,
become many starts of love,
as we fade into a crowd of faces
awaiting our bed?

My body grows pale with effort
into the milky dawn.
I succeed in acting one more day,
you already dressed and moving about,
a person with a coffee pot.
I stick out my tongue
to touch the brightening sky.

How do I know that tomorrow you will live?
Do you know how much you mean to me?
At the thought of your death
all thought stops in me,
I catch my breath.

Progress of Love

When I first met you I talked to your body,
avoided your eyes watching my next move,
to be prepared, not in hostility:
to be aware, to know my body.
I thought your eyes not human, watching;
and I was unhappy, drawn by their colorless
look, I myself suspect and your eyes a reproof,
until you spoke. Then body became an accent
of your voice. Your words delighted me,

you said simply the truth,
that with your interest each day existed,
and for that reason your body was.
Though I still love it,
that is because of you.

c. 1953

Marriage Song

As for life, I have not held a bouquet of roses
at your nose, nor slide scenes of the happy days.
My role has been the face machine planed,
slide slot of the lips, eyes sockets for ball bearings,
and tongue the emery stick of the motor.
You have had a city from me
who have moved through its cutting grooves,
the streets, and entered the offices and factories,
the rigid moulds, to come out beveled, shaped
and clean. Only my voice in its sharp edge
has protested; in the touch of your thought
upon me have you felt my love,
in reply cutting you. And you have wondered
for a place to keep such implement, in a house
of yielding chairs, spring mattresses and music;
and I too have wondered that somehow I had not been
returned in rack among other steel. My home,
my tool chest, does not shut out the light
or turn the key on me. I do not hang on a hook
like a hammer or nestle in a form like a plane
but stride about from room to room
to find a window from which to read
the saw-toothed buildings that cut us down to size;
and you beside me looking out. We meet here,
and I begin to soften, under a small tear
in your eye.

c. 1950

from Rescue the Dead *(1968)* 241

Oh Irene

What has happened to Irene whose bald brother
wore a wig? She asked me not to see her
and I loved her, which saddened her.
So sorry for herself, poor child,
working at Woolworth's where I would come.
She would grimace and ask me to leave.
The once she did let me walk her home after work
was to tell me of her brother's wig.
It was she felt ugly and unwanted
as she made plain she would live unhappily
because of him and did not want my love
to make her choice more difficult.
At her door, I left and slowly walked away,
ill about the wig, and unhappy for Irene
at Woolworth's where she would stand patiently
behind counter for customers. But it was not you
wearing the wig, Irene! Where are you?
Listen, I am through feeling unhappy.
I have been through for a long time!
I am grown up,
a man like your brother.

Against the Evidence

As I reach to close each book
lying open on my desk, it leaps up
to snap at my fingers. My legs
won't hold me, I must sit down.
My fingers pain me
where the thick leaves snapped together
at my touch.

All my life
I've held books in my hands
like children, carefully turning
their pages and straightening out

their creases. I use books
almost apologetically. I believe
I often think their thoughts for them.
Reading, I never know where theirs leave off
and mine begin. I am so much alone
in the world, I can observe the stars
or study the breeze, I can count the steps
on a stair on the way up or down,
and I can look at another human being
and get a smile, knowing
it is for the sake of politeness.
Nothing must be said of estrangement
among the human race and yet
nothing is said at all
because of that.
But no book will help either.
I stroke my desk,
its wood so smooth, so patient and still.
I set a typewriter on its surface
and begin to type
to tell myself my troubles.
Against the evidence, I live by choice.

An Omen

I love the bird that appears
each day at my window.
Whether the bird loves me
I only can surmise
from its regularity.

Six Movements on a Theme

(For Denise Levertov)

Thinking myself in a warm country
of maternal trees under whose shade
I lie and doze, I dream I am weightless.
Magnified faces stare back at me—
of friends wanting me to live
to whom I am dying stretched out
on the ground and barely breathing.
Dead, they say as I hold my breath
to close in and possess myself.

I dream my life to be a plant
floating upon a quiet pool,
gathering nourishment from water
and the sun. I emerge
of my own excess power, my roots
beginning to move like legs,
my leaves like arms,
the pistil the head. I walk
out of the pool
until I reach my utmost weariness
in a dance of the fading power
of my roots—when I lie down
silently to die and find myself
afloat again.

I see no fish crawling
to become man. The mountains
have been standing
without a single effort
to transform themselves
into castles or apartment houses.
Amid silence, I set a statue

in my image.
                    I love you, man,
on my knees. To you
I will address my pleas
for help. You will save me
from myself. From your silence
I will learn to live.

I was shown my only form.
I have no hope
but to approach myself,
palm touching palm.

Tapping on a wall
I feel my humankind,
secretly content
to suffer.
I too am a wall.

The stars are burning overhead.
Excited, I understand
from a distance:
I am fire,
I'll be dumb.

An Ontology

In the dark I step out of bed
and approaching the kitchen down the foyer
run my hand over the wall, smooth and rough
by turns, with cracks, holes, lumps
and dips the whole length,
my hand forming to each.
The floor bumpy and creaking,
now straight and now sagging,
the soles of my feet shape to each change.
My shoulders compress to the narrow hallway

as they go forward with me to the kitchen,
and there my eyes blink at the light.
Because I can find no direction of my own,
I eat. I belong with the bread, the milk
and the cheese. I become their peace.
I am nourished with myself
and go back to bed. I become the mattress,
I lie upon myself, I close my eyes,
I become sleep. It rolls me over
as I dream. I become a lack of control,
happening simultaneously everywhere.
It is me, I am happening.
As I move all moves with me.
I am this all as it moves
and harm cannot come unless I happen,
but because I exist, I am existence.

Secretly

My foot awes me,
the cushion of the sole
in profile shaped like a bird's head,
the toes long and narrow like a beak,
the arch to the foot
with the gentle incline
of a bird's body
and the heel thick and stubby
like a starling's tail.
In a slow motion it ascends
and descends in a half-circle,
tense, poised for flight.
The full weight of my body
today walking on it
supporting me in my weariness
it can perform its flight,
its shape delicate, light,
swift-seeming, tense and tireless

as I lie on a bed, my foot
secretly a bird.

Gardeners

So is the child slow stooping beside him
picking radishes from the soil.
He straightens up,
his arms full of the green leaves.
She bends low to each bunch and whispers,
Please come out big and red.
Tugs at them gently to give them time to change,
if they are moody and small.
Her arms filled, she paces
beside her grandfather's elderly puppet walk.

The Life Dance

I see bubbling out of the ground:
water, fresh, a pure smell. My mind
too begins to spring. I take
small hops. I enjoy myself
partly because I have the nerve.
Is anybody watching?
I care and don't care,
as I hop, and soon
because nobody is looking I'm leaping
and twisting into awkward shapes,
letting my hands make signs
of a meaning I do not understand.
I am absorbed in getting at what
till now
I had not been aware of.

There is a feeling in the world
I sometimes think I'm grasping.
I find myself holding a hand or
as I take a deep breath
I think it is there.

Three in Transition

(For WCW)

I wish I understood the beauty
in leaves falling. To whom
are we beautiful
as we go?

I lie in the field
still, absorbing the stars
and silently throwing off
their presence. Silently
I breathe and die
by turns.

He was ripe
and fell to the ground
from a bough
out where the wind
is free
of the branches.

For My Daughter in Reply to a Question

We're not going to die,
we'll find a way.
We'll breathe deeply
and eat carefully.

We'll think always on life.
There'll be no fading for you or for me.
We'll be the first
and we'll not laugh at ourselves ever
and your children will be my grandchildren.
Nothing will have changed
except by addition.
There'll never be another as you
and never another as I.
No one ever will confuse you
nor confuse me with another.
We will not be forgotten and passed over
and buried under the births and deaths to come.

The Hope

In the woods as the trees fade in the dusk
I am unable to speak or to gesture.
I lie down to warm myself against the ground.
If I live through the night
I will be a species
related to the tree
and the cold dark.

Night at an Airport

Just as the signal tower lights flash
on and off, so the world recedes
and comes on, giving the illusion
of end and beginning. Before light
there was darkness in which the plane
kept roaring in for landing. Particles
of dust rise in the wind's path
and settle obscurely
when the wind has passed.

We have our beginnings
in breeze or storm, dancing or swirling;
and are still when the wind is still.
We have earth and return to it—
everlasting as a thought.

c. 1940

Anew

Dante forgot to say,
Thank you, Lord, for sending me
to hell. I find myself happier
than when I was ignorant.
I am left helpless
but more cheerful.
Nothing could be worse
than to start ignorant again.
And so I look to you
to help me love my life
anew.

Walk There

(For Marianne Moore)

The way through the woods is past trees,
touching grass, bark, stone, water and mud;
into the night of the trees, beneath
their damp cold, stumbling on roots,
discovering no trail, trudging
and smelling pine, cypress and musk.
A rabbit leaps across my path,
and something big rustles in the bush.
Stand still, eye the nearest tree
for climbing. Subside in fear
in continued silence. Walk.

See the sky splattered with leaves.
Ahead, is that too the sky
or a clearing?
Walk there.

PART TEN

New Poems of the 1960's

Brief Cases

It was then that carrying brief cases
was prohibited in public as a mark
of impotence; no man need disgrace himself,
not recognizing his own shortcomings,
obvious to others, especially police
who carried their nightsticks
in their hands.
                    "What are men if not men,"
was the motto they wore on their caps
in red and white, with scarves twirled
around their throats, of any color
for their pride. And the women,
oh the women, were unhappy.

It was then that carrying brief cases
in public was prohibited to them too,
for in these brief cases were tiny men
packed neatly in small cartons
to be opened in private homes.
Oh the little men danced on the tables
and kissed the lips of the women
who gave their lips to be kissed,
and the tall men who carried the brief cases
withdrew into the dark rooms of the houses.

Oh the women were not happy
but the tiny men grew tall
and all brief cases were abolished
and replaced by beds
that were then carried on the strong backs
of the tall men who once were little.
Oh the women were not happy,
nor the tall men with all the little habits
of the past
                    How did it all end?
I'm hard put to tell you but I did hear
that the women chose to live

and the once little men and those
withdrawn into the dark
gave birth.

Versicle and Response

    Look smooth
    talk nice
    stay happy—

    Kiss my ass

    They put a telephone in his coffin
    with an outside extension
    and were not surprised
    when the receiver was lifted
    and there were sighing sounds:
    Hair growing? Skin shrinking?
    Larvae coming into being?
    When those above asked for an answer
    they received none and went down
    and opened the grave. They found
    the receiver back in its cradle.

    This happened over and over
    until one man decided to stay down
    beside the coffin and peek through
    a hole bored in the wood.
    The sounds were repeated,
    the receiver lifted from its rest.
    The answer to the question from above
    was those sighing sounds again.
    And when they brought up the man
    for his observations

he stared long at his colleagues
and said finally, as if to himself,
I am a mystery.

First Coffin Poem

I love you, my plain pine box,
because you also are a bench,
with the lid down. Can you see
my friends in a row seated
at ease with themselves?
I am in a coffin
and it has been set against the wall
of a living room. It is just before
dinner and several friends are standing
about with glasses in their hands,
drinking to the possibilities
that life offers.
                    The coffin also
could be placed as a table
in front of a grand sofa, with food
and drinks served on it, and an ashtray.

It would be so much simpler, less gruesome
to use an actual coffee table, you say,
or a real bench, but ah, that would prove
how rigid we must be about ourselves
and cause us to languish, caught
in a limitation. We must make one thing
do for another.
                    I am hope, in urging you
to use my pine box. Take me to your home
when I die imperceptibly. Without fuss
place me against the wall in my coffin,
a conversation piece, an affirmation of change.
I am, sincerely, yours.

I Don't Want To

I have such a sympathy for my floor
with its varied shades of brown, its grain
of graceful arcs and swirls lying there
to be admired and stepped on.
I do not want to be a floor,
I do not want to be stepped on,
nails driven into, I do not want to lie
silently and brood at night in the silence
and emptiness around and above me.
I do not want this pity either
that I have for the floor.
I do not want admiration,
especially for my silence and dedication
as a floor.

   Moreover, I do not want to be
cut down and removed from where I was born
and raised. I do not want to miss the rain
and wind. I do not want to miss growing old,
revered and enjoyed by people camping beneath me.
I don't want to miss their voices and their words
of pleasure in the cool shade and I do not want
to miss the nights of roaming bear and puma
rubbing their hides against my bark
and time happening, feeling myself begin to rot
away, knowing my life was full.

        I don't want
to miss dropping my seed that would grow
in my place. What a marvelous feeling
to belong for always, that I shall never cease
and never depart from these woods, given to me
in which to grow and be reborn.

I don't want to be a floor.
What then could I think of myself,
what then could I make of my life?
I would sag and fall into the basement.
Don't ask my why. I'd fall even though

I were new, strong, fresh-sawed planks
of uniform size.

An Old Man Looks at the Young Kissing

The yearning to make it all there is
to life, their lips so painfully curled
around that thought.

Feeling with My Hands

Will this poem be able to think and breathe
and have sex? Will it be able
to lift a finger to call a waiter
for the menu? Will it have hopes
of a future life? Will it have friends
among other poems? Oh yes, will it
be able to write other poems?

I do not want it to rest on its merits.
I want others to look through it
to see me breathing and taking food
and embracing my wife, telling her
she has lovely teeth. This poem
should have an erection and everywhere
should say hello and be a friend
and not hesitate to tell other poems
what it thinks about them. Be pleasant
but be truthful. Be happy but fear not death.
Here it is and I am still talking
and feeling with my hands.

While I Live

I dream of language as the sun.
I whisper to that plant
whose own language is the wind.
It cups its flower to listen
at the wind's pressure and we talk
together of the darkness in language:
what Dante suffered at its command—
only that I may endure the necessary
ecstasy of my personal death.

I want my trees to love me
and my grass to reach up to the porch
where I am no one but the end of time,
as I stand waiting for renewal in my brain,
because I am what the sun shines forth:
I am labor, I am a disposition to live.
Who dies? Only the sun
but you must wait
while I live.

Morning

I am not a bird
as I open my eyes to the daylight
and examine their wings and their beaks.
I am not their flesh and they sing.
Brain, call me what you will,
my identity is with you
as I listen with the ear you give me
and see with the eyes you activate.
I am a creature, given this word,
who, told to, walks on two legs.
(Is that what they are?)
I have arms. (What are arms?)
I am thankful I exist. (What does that mean,

brain?) All these words,
where have I learned to know them
as quickly as you think them?
Should I not be proud
as pleasure rises in my chest
at the thought that suits the word?
I will be proud (what now is "proud"?)
I am too delighted to reject what delights me.
I am too far out of myself, beyond silence,
to return. I am a talker, hearing myself
and replying to myself. I have a companion
and I am on my feet,
walking where I can be heard.
The birds fall silent,
the road between the woods leading somewhere,
sending its emptiness ahead.

Silent birds, are you listening to my voice
giving me my self? Are you recording
your listening to me? Are you birds then?
And when will you sing again?
My brain will have birds to record itself
and it falls silent, my voice halts.
There is silence
and I could fade again.

They live, I live,
they sing, I hear them sing.
No, this is not happiness.
It is the beginning,
it is curiousity,
it is touch, by ear.
It is sight,
it is a coincidence of brain and body.
I can be happy
in this knowledge.

Waiting Inside

I protest my isolation
but protest is a mark of my defeat,
even as I write.
                Being a victim,
I am an accuser. Being human,
others feels my fallen weight
upon their thoughts and are oppressed—
as I am, their guilt unlike mine
and unrelated and without hope in it
of change for me.
                Guilty, my oppressor
and I go separate ways
though we could relieve each other
by going together, as Whitman wrote,
with our arms around each other's waists,
in support.